CULTIVATING THE PRESENCE

CULTIVATING THE PRESENCE

A SPIRITUAL GUIDE FOR
A JOURNEY TOWARD
THE PRESENCE OF GOD

the Reverend Tom Sampson

Thomas Y. Crowell Company
Established 1834
New York

Copyright Acknowledgments are in the back of the book

Manufactured in the United States of America

LIBRARY OF CONGRESS CATALOGING IN PUBLICATION DATA
Sampson, Tom.
    Cultivating the presence.
    Bibliography: p.
    Includes index.
    1. Spiritual life.   2.   Devotional literature.
I. Title.
BV4501.2.S17   248'.4   76-27316
ISBN 0-690-01205-5
ISBN 0-690-01206-3(pbk.)

1 2 3 4 5 6 7 8 9 10

AUTHOR'S ACKNOWLEDGMENTS

A resource book such as this could not have been written without the advice and counsel of many colleagues in Christian ministry. Special mention must be given to: Dr. Edward Bergstraesser, Dr. Dale Brown, Rev. Gordon Collier, Rev. James Duren, Dr. Arthur Ellersieck, Rev. Robert Frederick, Dr. Porter French, Rev. Edward Goltz, Rev. John Hubner, Dr. Clyde Manschreck, Rev. Donald Stoner, Rev. David Wheeler, Mrs. Raymond Mons, Mrs. Maxwell Yahr, and Mrs. Robert Wagner. I am indebted to Mrs. Helen Dortmann and Mrs. Betty Hill for help in typing and to my wife, Eleanor, for patience and support.

To you—who are seekers;
To you—young and old
  who have toiled all night and caught nothing
But who want to launch out into the deeps
  and let down your nets for a draught;

I want to speak as simply, as tenderly,
  as clearly as I can.

For God can be found.
There is a last rock for your souls,
A resting place of absolute peace
  and joy and power
  and radiance and security.

There is a Divine Center
  in which your life can slip,
A new and absolute orientation in God;
A Center where you live with Him
  and out of which you see all of life,
Through new and radiant vision,
  tinged with sorrow and pangs,
  new joys, unspeakable
  and full of Glory.

Thomas R. Kelly*

*Thomas R. Kelly, *A Testament of Devotion,* Introduction by Douglas Steere (New York: Harper & Bros., 1941), pp. 18–19.

Brother Lawrence

He was the best-known scrubber and washer of pots and pans the world has ever seen. He spent many years in a monastery kitchen, but great men traveled hundreds of miles to visit him and listen to his counsel. He never wrote a book, yet multitudes of people have been spiritually guided by him. After his death, his fellow monks gathered together some of his writings and letters. They published them in a small pamphlet which, in honor of his spirit, they titled *The Practice of the Presence of God*. It has become one of the great Christian classics of devotional literature.

Nicholas Herman was born in Lorraine, France, in 1611, of peasant parents. He grew up with little formal education, but his meditative spirit attracted him to people who introduced him to life and religion. When he was thirty years old, he had to serve in the professional army of France at the beginning of the Thirty Years' War. He was severely wounded in battle, which proved to be a blessing because his long recuperation allowed him time to seek a way of life more suitable to his reflective nature. In 1666, at the age of fifty-five, he became a lay brother in the Reformed Carmelite Order in Paris.

For fifteen years, Brother Lawrence, as he was called as a monk, worked in the kitchen. He described himself as "a great awkward fellow who broke everything." When his superiors sent him overseas to purchase provisions and wine, he said he "could not go about the boat except by rolling himself over the casks." If Brother Lawrence lacked physical abilities, he more than made up for it in spiritual talents. He had an inner spirit of peace, patience, faithfulness, industry, hope, and Christian love. He not only experienced the Presence, he sincerely practiced it.

As Brother Lawrence had found such an advantage in walking in the Presence of God, it was natural to recommend it to others, but his example was a stronger inducement than any arguments he could propose.... It was observed that in the greatest hurry of business in the kitchen, he still preserved his recollection and heavenly-mindedness. He was never hasty or loitering, but did each thing in its season, with an even uninterrupted composure and tranquility of spirit. "That time of business" said he "does not with me differ from the time of prayer, and in the noise and clatter of my kitchen, while several persons are at the same time calling for different things, I possess God in as great tranquility as if I were upon my knees at the blessed sacrament."*

*Brother Lawrence, *The Practice of the Presence of God* (New York: Revell, 1895), 4th Conversation.

Brother Lawrence died in 1691, but his unusual awareness of the Presence of God lives on today. Over the past three hundred years, the small collection of his writings has continued to be read and reread by those seeking the Presence. The book *The Practice of the Presence of God* is of sublime simplicity. It is an authentic example of the cultivation of the Presence.

A NOTE TO THE READER

What Is the Presence?

The Presence is the experience of the God, the Creator, in each of us.

The experience of the Presence fills the mind with thanksgiving, overwhelms the soul with fullness of joy, and satisfies the heart with inner singing.

The experience of the Presence of God is *the* memorable event of a lifetime; often life-changing and always unforgettable. The apostle Paul had a great experience of the Presence, on the road to Damascus, when he heard the voice of Jesus, and it changed his life. On the other hand, George Fox had repeated experiences of the Presence, as we shall see. Time and again he heard a voice, or saw a vision, or had an opening, or saw a Light Within. Each occasion was, to him, the Presence of God. Each event deepened his commitment to Christ.

The Presence is the awareness of a powerful Force beyond self . . . a sense of being in touch with God's Plan . . . a freedom from guilt and fear of the past . . . an awareness of being accepted by God in spite of our human failings.

Every man and every woman finds a new and deeper peace when the Presence comes. Once it has visited, the occasion is forever cherished. The event is so sublime, it is almost beyond words.

> By the Presence we are searched and known.
> From it there is no escape, either in heaven or hell.
> It follows us all the days of our lives.
> In it we find an inner security, even in the face of our
>   enemies.
> By it we have an assurance of the love of God.
> The Presence drops the scales
>   of spiritual blindness from our eyes.
> It brings the redirection of living.
> The Presence is the breath of Eternal Life.

The Ongoing Search for the Presence

In our time, men and women are seeking the Presence of God in a wide variety of ways. Some practice mental and physical disciplines with Oriental mystics. Others become devoted disciples of foreign gurus. A few dress in unusual costumes, eat strange foods, and study ancient dogmas. Many join small encounter groups and house churches. Some concentrate on exacting methods of meditation. Quite a few are captivated by self-appointed saviors. A great many are looking to the Church for new experiences with the Spirit.

No matter which religious group you may join, there are some fundamentals about the cultivation of the Presence of God of which you should be aware. There are procedures that have been developed by many of the most outstanding Christians of history.

There are specific *ways to begin* your spiritual discoveries.

There are decisions to be made about *how much time* you ought to spend on your search.

There are *particular attitudes that you will need* in order to make progress.

There are *dangers to avoid.*

There are special *books of spiritual counsel.*

There are *recognized Christians whom you should emulate.*

How This Book Can Help You

This book is for those men and women who hope that the Presence of God will become a more real and active part of their lives. It is for those persons who want to live more creatively and more meaningfully and who are willing to allow the Presence of God to bring that about through judgment, support, forgiveness, and direction.

This book is for those who recognize that the Presence of God can never be commanded but who have faith that It can be personally cultivated.

This book is a survey and summary of what the well-known spiritual-life authorities of Christian history have advised concerning the cultivation of the Presence. These advisers come from all centuries and many areas of Christian faith: Roman Catholic and Protestant: Franciscan and Jesuit; Anglican, Baptist, Lutheran, Methodist, and Quaker, as well as from the nondenominational churches.

This Book Is a Guide and Resource

This book is a guide for those who are just beginning, as well as a resource book for those who have been on the spiritual journey for a long time.

Cultivating the Presence brings the Presence alive in a number of ways:

it begins with several personal experiences from the life of the author;

it then describes six ways by which the Presence makes Itself known;

it illustrates the methods by which every person can cultivate the Presence;

it presents characteristic excerpts from twenty-one of the best-known books of the Presence;

it reviews forty-two spiritual-life books that are considered classics in the field;

it includes short biographies of the authors;

it concludes with an editorial about the Presence in society today.

CONTENTS

INTRODUCTION

MY EXPERIENCES
WITH THE
PRESENCE

A.

Until I was twenty-eight years old, I refused to have anything to do with religion. I had been in a church only twice, both times at the urging of a friend. During these years, I remember saying that I would "never be seen, even dead, in a church." My father was a successful executive who ridiculed prayer as well as the religious believer. He felt all the work of the world was done by business people.

My first steady job was in a brokerage house, which sold stocks and bonds. I enjoyed being with people who were investing and speculating, but I observed, on becoming friends with some customers, that their increased income did not necessarily solve their personal problems. All too often, shaky marriages, alcoholism, or destructive anxieties seemed to grow worse as incomes grew larger. I continued to talk stocks, but I could not forget the personal stories. Gradually my interest in the business waned.

During this period of my life I was living alone in a strange city, so I began attending church on the lonely weekends. I went back again and again because a minister there kept providing me with new insights into my life. I also felt the warm welcome of church members. I gave more and more spare time to the church's activities. They were heartening alternatives to what I felt were the objectives of speculating in securities. I reconsidered religion. It seemed to me to be dealing with the meaningful questions about the purpose of life.

I quit my job and enrolled in a school of social work. That, I felt, would meet my interest in people. But I soon discovered I was wrong. I found social workers were doing important things for people, often in a material way of obtaining aid and solving financial crises, but I didn't find them dealing with the basic attitudes and convictions about the purpose of life. How would people really change if they did not think through their values, their goals and the meanings of existence?

Within a year, I had entered a school of theology. In another year, I had become a student-minister of a struggling inner-city mission church in the Pilsen area of Chicago.

Although I was now satisfied that religion, after all, was going to be my career, everything was not so clear about my personal life. I had a deep inferiority complex, coming perhaps from the fact that I was the only child of divorced parents. I also found it most uncomfortable to relate to women. Sexuality was a matter to which I was deeply drawn but didn't know what to do about. I also was extremely success-oriented in a very materialistic way (I wanted to be top dog) and was insensitive to the world of feelings and emotions. I fought those battles every day. I became frustrated with myself and didn't understand why I could not throw off inferiority, sexual insecurity, and an insatiable desire for personal recognition. It also seemed that the more I studied at the seminary, the more conscious I became of my personal problems. At times the struggles became almost unbearable. I knew what Paul was talking about when he wrote that the spirit was willing but the flesh was weak.

It was in a very confused state of mind that I went to a summer conference for more religious training. While there, I made the opportunity to talk frequently with an older colleague about my personal problems. He counseled me for a long time. However, I still didn't feel any stronger.

One day a friend invited me to help with a worship service at a distant church-in-the-woods where tourists gathered. When we arrived, I found a small chapel of hand-hewn logs. Inside were homemade pews and a pulpit. An old upright piano was the only other piece of furniture.

My part in the morning service was to read the Scripture. The passage was from Isaiah and concluded with the well-known words "though your sins be as scarlet, they can become as white as snow." After reading them, I was prepared to hear the message for the day.

But I never heard a word of it. For, in an instant, almost as soon as I had sat down, a strange sensation came over me. I felt suddenly caught up in some powerful grasp. The words I had just read swept over and through me. Although I knew they were hundreds of years old, nevertheless they seemed written just for me. I sat transfixed. Though I heard no voice, I had the most positive feeling that what I had read was directed right at me. As I sat in that small chapel, I felt a great burden lifted from my shoulders, a strange emotion of utter relief and of great acceptance.

Now, many years later, I can still relive exactly where I sat on that Sunday morning, on that wooden platform in that log church. I remember vividly how I felt then. It was as if some unknown power came into my being, surrounding, comforting, and possessing me. I felt the grip of my sinful life gone.

I do not claim that all my problems were solved, or that I have never been bothered since with inferiority or sexuality and other anxieties since then. I have. But certainly not to the same degree. And I know now that I am not alone in fighting them.

At that time, I did not know what had really happened to me, but now, after much thought and reflection, I conclude that I had a mystical experience. It took place quietly and so forcefully that it has remained indelibly imprinted on my memory. I had been visited by a Power which was unseen but very real. I know it for a fact. No one can convince me otherwise, nor take the feeling or the memory of it away. I now know what others are talking about when they relate similar events.

What I had not found through confession and therapy with my counselor, I received unexpectedly from the Presence.

This incident is, of course, special to me and always will remain so. But it is really not an unusual experience. Thousands of persons testify to events very much like mine. Month after month, religious magazines are filled with such testimonies. I merely rejoice that I can add my witness to that of so many others. I rejoice, too, because the experience in the woods that summer has sustained me and inspired me ever since. It enabled me to overcome some of my personal problems and grow toward more maturity in the ministry. I went on to several pastorates in the years which followed with a clearer mind and heart.

B.

Many years ago, there was an infrequent visitor at my house. It was present only on special occasions, a pleasant addition to friendly gatherings. My "guest" was the social drink, the after-work cocktail. It seemed a natural way of entertaining. Most people expected it and everybody seemed to be doing it.

As time passed, I discovered additional ways of using

Scotch-and-sodas. I found them helpful to counteract the fatigue of the end of the day, or even a discouraging time at the office. I discovered they could supply exhilaration, even though temporary, in the face of loneliness. I learned they could afford me a way of escaping from my problems.

So the years went by for others in ordinary fashion but, for me, the pleasure of the occasional drink settled into a pattern. Once in a while I would have too much and would regret it on the following day but I knew I could handle what I was doing. I agreed that liquor was not really helping me but it seemed the lesser of evils and I continued.

I cannot tell you when I felt I should throw off the habit. I only know I found it impossible to do so. I tried every device I knew to kill its hold on me. I put a black dot on each week I thought I had had too much as Benjamin Franklin did with his problem, whatever it was. I tried making resolutions on special occasions. I consulted friends. I poured liquor down the sink. I tried prayer and renewed commitment to God. Some of these helped but only for a while. Soon I would be back in the grip of the drink-syndrome.

I began to observe seriously that liquor had become more a part of my career than I really wanted. I saw, too, how often my habit was deceiving me. Relationships with friends were being clouded. I felt my health was not as it should be. I was losing time that I should be spending more clearly on my work.

Sometimes I would think of the Presence. It had come into my life once before. Where was It now? Did It really exist? Had God deserted my prayers? What could I do to find help?

Then I came to the time when I had more serious bouts with what had come to be an enemy, and the day came when

I knew that I had lost the battle with my own self. I knew I was defeated. I was aware that something else was in control of my life. I fell into despondency and can vividly recall the darkness of those terrible days. I would cry out in despair, "God, help me, help me, help me." Anguish and remorse swept back and forth across my soul. Hour upon hour and day after day I cried, "Help me, someone help me." Yet I actually did not expect an answer. I knew I was beaten. Who could help? Who could help me with my own soul? God, too, seemed far away.

Finally those days of darkness passed, of course, but I can still feel, after all these intervening years, the fear I had about the future. I knew I would soon be in the battle again. But a week went by and there was no desire to drink. Then two weeks passed, and then three. I could hardly believe it. What had happened? The weeks stretched into months. Had the Presence really killed the problem? I began to feel elated and filled with a new confidence in myself. I experienced a great inner joy of victory. I had won. I had thrown off the Great Deceiver. He was not able to control me anymore.

Now, as I tell you this after many many years, I am still impressed with what happened at that time. I still do not completely understand all that went on. All I know is that in some mysterious way I was saved from a recurring habit that I had not been able to overcome by my own resolutions, determination, or prayers. Some power had come into my life to change me. It had come without announcement, fanfare, or dramatics.

Today I am not sorry I had that battle with alcohol. It has served to remind me how fragile human nature can often be. I know something of the tenacious grip and daily temptations which may face other persons. I have been there. Like Paul, I have experienced the time when I "did not understand my own actions," when I "did those things I did not want to do," and when I could "will what is right but could not do it." Like Paul and many other persons, I know what it means to cry out in despair, "Who will deliver me from this body of death?"

But I also know, through my failure and sin, what it means to exclaim in thankfulness, "Thanks be to God who gives us the victory!" For certainly it was not I, but the Presence, that gave me back my self and my freedom.

C.

I found that the two suburban parishes I served were exciting. In each of them I worked with well-educated, sophisticated people who had outstanding qualities of leadership and management. Both congregations grew in size and both built new sanctuaries for worship and rooms for religious education.

I spent thirty years in the two parishes. But gradually I grew restless and unhappy. I felt something was lacking. It seemed as though everyone, including myself, was more interested in numerical growth and program activity than in confronting the controversial problems of the times: racism, poverty, and injustice. I had preached that being a Christian meant caring for the oppressed, but I knew that I should do more than just talk, or even help plan additional church events. What should I do? Where should I go?

I began looking at different kinds of ministries. I wanted a congregation no one else would take. I prayed for a difficult parish where my faith could be tested.

One day an Italian cobbler with a broken English accent phoned my suburban parsonage to ask if I would serve a small, poor, inner-city church. I accepted with excitement. The church proved to be composed of a disintegrating congregation in a dying part of Chicago; an old German neighborhood, surrounded on the south by a black ghetto, on the east by an expanding Spanish barrio, and on the west by wornout factories. Every social agency had long since deserted the area, as gangs, vandalism, and community disorganization had taken their toll.

I soon discovered, also, that the decay of the neighborhood had infected the members of the church (most of whom were elderly) with hopelessness. They were divided into several factions and angrily blamed each other for the decline of membership. Their continual bickering was so divisive that many additional members had left or fled to more reasonable congregations.

The conflicts within that congregation appeared in many forms. Meetings that had been called to discuss the possible future of the church ended in the chaos of shouting and uncontrolled anger, as minority younger groups struggled for dominance over the conservative elderly majority. Prejudices and hatreds, bred within the congregation by years of conflict, were impossible to counteract. Even efforts of outsiders to help the church plan its future were met with antagonism.

The real depth of hopelessness was not always revealed in such obvious ways. More often it showed itself in emotional and psychological abuse. I was often called names and publicly insulted. My efforts to initiate new solutions so threatened the minority leaders they reacted with more attacks. When I tried to bring about reconciliation, my suggestions were interpreted as weakness. Once I was considered weak, the attacks on me became even more blatant.

Most of the people in the congregation were caring and

honorable. But these did not have influence. It was the few caught up in the power struggle who ruined any future the church might have had.

As I recall this atmosphere of harassment, I am well aware that such difficulties are common to many ministers. I remember the persecutions which our Lord had to suffer. I know they were far greater than any I had to bear and His love is an inspiration to me. I learned a lot about myself and I do not regret the four years I served that inner-city parish, though those years were filled with frustration, worry, sleepless nights, and bitter disappointment. What is unusual about this story is what happened to my spirit.

When the anger and hatred first began, I reacted with hurt pride. I became upset, I lost my cool. But as they continued, I made a significant discovery. The harassment was forcing me to rethink my own beliefs. How was a person who was trying to be a Christian expected to act under such circumstances? What was the mystery of returning love for hatred, good for evil? What was the healing capacity of forgiveness, patience, prayer?

As I tried to respond in these Christian ways (and I often failed) I discovered spiritual strengths I never knew I had. I found the more wildly I was attacked, the more inner security I developed. It seemed as though a Presence, that same Presence I had felt so many years before, was with me again.

Furthermore, I became aware that most of the congregation was silently watching the harassment. But I did not feel justified in asking them to take sides. I returned always to my own inner spiritual resources. I concluded that the way I responded to the situation was going to say a great deal to the members about the Christian faith. My reaction had the power to reveal more about the importance of my beliefs than any words I might preach on Sunday.

As the years passed, and the slander continued, I discovered I could actually look forward to the encounters. I found them proving-grounds for my deepening faith. They helped me understand more of the words of Psalm 23: "Thou preparest a table before me in the presence of my enemies."

After a while, I even learned that I could silently thank my persecutors. I could pray for them at the same time they were threatening me. I could give thanks because I knew it was their hatred which helped me find a Power that gave me unexpected strength.

Finally, the membership voted to sell the church building. Because of the change in the city and neighborhood, the members had declined from almost one thousand men and women to two dozen worshipers. They planned to join neighborhood parishes. I felt my efforts were finished. The unhappy situation had, however, given me a new and deeper awareness of the abiding support of the Presence. For that I gave thanks. It would make me a better minister for the future.

As I look back upon the dark years of that pastorate, I know I lost many battles to selfishness and prejudice. But I won a new respect for my own soul. I had often read how historic Christians experienced a Presence which sustained them in their time of trial. I now have an understanding of what they discovered.

D.

The Presence aided me once again, several years ago, when I was fired from my administrative job at a midwestern college. I had studied at the school when I was younger, so I had undertaken the work with much enthusiasm. In fact, I had served in a number of volunteer capacities for the institution, and I had been a regular contributor as well as a member of their Board of Directors. But a year after I began work there, a new administration took office and within several months, I was advised that my "services would no longer be needed."

Being fired was a terrible blow for me. I felt betrayed. I was angry and felt rejected.

I recall this incident not to protest being fired—that's nothing new; people are often dismissed—but to report that, after being let go, an extraordinary thing happened to my soul.

The day I was told of my termination, I left my office feeling very bitter. I planned never to return even though I had a contract to the end of the term. I did not sleep that night. The next day I spent composing a letter to student and faculty friends explaining why I would not be seeing them again.

But the pain of dismissal from my own school, which I had so long supported, overwhelmed me even as I wrote. I wondered what advice my best friends would give me, so I called several persons on the phone. One suggested that I leave right away. Another advised, "If you resign immediately, consider the pay you will lose. Bluff your way through even if you don't do any work." Another replied, "You'll get over it. Go back to the job as soon as you can." I was grateful for their advice but, like the situation with Job in the Old Testament, none of the observations by friends really "spoke" to me. I continued in my despair.

When night came, I tried to sleep but was kept awake by

my soul-searching. What should I do? About two in the morning, I had a very strange experience. My mind stopped debating with itself and was filled, instead, with the story of Peter and his defense of Christ. In that incident, Peter draws his sword in violent reaction to those who are threatening Jesus. The story became immediately real to me. I saw Jesus put out His hand as if to say, "Peter, that is not the way."

Suddenly my own situation became clearer. I was reacting violently to threats against what I loved, my job and my school. I was trying to strike back by being revengeful, as Peter had been when he drew his sword. Then, in those early morning hours, I felt the spirit of Christ say very forcefully to me, "That's not the way. Put up your resentment."

This faint light of insight entered my spiritual darkness of anger and began to grow with the returning light of day. By daybreak I had considered going back to my job, for the few remaining months I would have of it, to show that faith could overcome the tremendously strong power of resentment.

My new outlook was still very tender and shaky when I went to my church that Sunday morning. It needed confirmation, so I shared my inner battle with the congregation. "On previous occasions, I have tried to speak to your problems," I explained. "Now I ask you to help me with mine." Thinking the matter through aloud with these witnesses helped confirm my new resolve.

But I was in for still another surprise. During that Sunday, only forty-eight hours after I had been so desperately angry and bitter, my regained faith gradually turned another corner. It became aggressive love. Instead of being led to accept gracefully what had happened, I now eagerly looked forward to returning to work. I realized that the defeating action of my employer was not as important as the mastery of my own self. I was a new man. I had found freedom from self in the capacity to love. I rejoiced in the power.

I had lost a good job. Who hasn't? The point is not that I lost a job but that I found the Presence. Something came into my heart and completely turned my attitude around within the space of a few hours. It moved me to a change against my will. A day after determining that I would not return, I was acting in exactly the opposite way. Being dismissed brought me a soul-shaking experience. I was visited by a power that must have been the Presence. The impact of this new experience, which struck me in such a brief span of time and to such depth, will remain with me long after the loss of the job is entirely forgotten.

I have included these experiences with the Presence not because I believe they are unusual. To the contrary, you have only to pick up one of the numerous daily devotional guides, published by many religious organizations, to read how God and the Presence constantly reveal themselves in the lives of everyday people. I have added my testimonies to support the intention that this book should not be just another resource *about* the Presence but, rather, that it might become a book *of* the Presence. I pray that you may not just be reading about the revelation of the Presence as you read this book, but that you may be experiencing It; not necessarily in the ways I did, but in a fashion important to your own development of faith.

As I have described, I have felt the Presence in several

different situations. It originally broke into my life, as I sat in that small forest-chapel, and released me from the conviction of personal sin. It came again and healed me of a deepening habit that I had not been able to overcome by my own efforts. Then, many years after that, I felt It in my life as I found inner strength to meet hatred and persecution with patience and love. And It came at still another time and in another form, when It taught me how to change my violent reaction at being fired to a response of acceptance and peace.

The Presence rarely, if ever, comes in the same way to different people. It came to *me* as forgiveness of sin, healing of my brokenness, strengthening of faith, and finally, redirection of faith. It can come to *you* in these or many other ways. Let us turn, in the first chapter, to what some of these ways may be.

1

EXPLANATIONS
OF THE
PRESENCE

The experience of the Presence rarely happens twice in the same way. Each occasion is surrounded with different circumstances and emotions. However, when many of the happenings are summarized, they appear to fall into a number of general categories. For example, I note at least six major attributes of the Presence.

1. It is a personal experience.
2. It is a state of inner security.
3. It is really inescapable.
4. It directly intervenes in our lives.
5. It is part of our basic nature.
6. It calls us to share life with others.

First, the Presence Is
a Personal Experience

All of the well-known religious persons to whom we shall refer in this book have testified, in one way or another, to occasions when the Presence of God appeared in their lives. Some of their stories are more dramatic than others, but all agree that the Presence is a personal experience.

Francis of Assisi grew up in the home of well-to-do parents who wished him to study law, or follow the family business of merchants in cloth. But Francis became interested in the Church and, much to the displeasure of his father, spent many hours in prayer. One day, while praying in Assisi, he was sure he heard a voice from the crucifix say to him: "Go, Francis, and repair my house, which is in ruins." Francis hurried home, took a good deal of the cloth from his father's prosperous store, and sold it for the benefit of the Church. His father had him arrested and later brought before the bishop. This harassment made Francis even more determined to fulfill the command he had heard. In the presence of all, he took off most of his clothes, gave them to his father, renounced his family and the world, and announced he would henceforth give his whole life to repairing the Church.

Certainly, for Francis, the Presence was a personal event. So directly personal, in fact, that It came between him and his family. So utterly personally convincing, that It changed the direction of his life.

Another illustration of the Presence, and Its appearance in a personal way, comes from the life of George Fox, the founder of the Society of Friends (Quakers).

George Fox was born of poor parents in England in 1624. He left home, at the age of nineteen, to search for answers to many religious questions that were bothering his life. Later, writing in 1647, he tells of his first religious experience, which took place after several years of his wandering. "When all my hopes . . . were gone, so that I had nothing outwardly to help me, nor could tell what to do, then, O then, I heard a voice which said, 'There is one, even Jesus Christ, that can speak to thy condition,' and when I heard it, my heart did leap for joy."

Fox continued to have many other personal religious experiences, all of which convinced him that there was a mysterious Power which could guide those who cultivated it. He called it the "Light Within." In fact, so many others began to experience the leadings and the healings of the Light Within that they formed themselves into what they called the Society of Friends, or Quakers.

Francis of Assisi, George Fox, and many others have found the Presence to be a very personal event. Let it suffice to summarize this claim with these sentences from William Wordsworth's "Lines Composed a Few Miles Above Tintern Abbey":

> And I have felt
> A presence that disturbs me, with joy
> Of elevated thoughts, a sense sublime
> Of something far more deeply interfused . . . .

Second, the Presence Is a State of Inner Security

By "Presence" I mean a special condition of mind or soul. It is a state of Grace; that is, an awareness that you have been accepted by God, in spite of what you may have done. For example, the Prodigal Son found a condition of Grace upon being accepted back by his father, who loved him, forgave him, and took him in, in spite of the wasteful life he had been living.

Grace is a feeling of knowing that you are forgiven. It is a spirit of thankfulness. It is a peace of mind. It is a sense of inner serenity, even though surrounding circumstances may be hostile and difficult. For example, the psalmist who wrote Psalm 23 knew the inner security of the Presence when he penned the line: "Thou preparest a table before me, in the presence of my enemies." The psalmist knew the state of being inwardly secure even though outwardly surrounded by danger.

Elsewhere the psalmists speak of the inner peace which comes from the presence of the Presence.

In Thy Presence is fullness of Joy. 16:11

Come before His Presence with singing. 100:2

Tremble, O earth, at the Presence
of the Lord, at the Presence of
the God of Jacob. 114:7

The upright shall dwell in the
Presence. 140:13

Elijah the Tishbite stood on Mount Horeb in the midst of
the wind, earthquake, and fire. Then he heard the "still
small voice," "wrapped his face in his mantle and went out
and stood at the entrance to the cave" (see I Kings 19:9–15).
Wherever this story is retold, there are multitudes who believe that for Elijah this was a supreme moment of inner
peace and security in the Presence of the Lord.

In another story from the Old Testament, we hear of
courageous young David striding forth to meet the oversized
armored Goliath in an individual battle to decide the larger
confrontation of the Philistine army against the men of Is-
rael. Certainly David must have had the security and inner
strength of faith with him when he said to his adversary,
"You come to me with a sword and with a spear but I come
to you in the name of the Lord of hosts" (see I Samuel
17:1–54).

In like manner, the awareness of the inner security of the
Presence has supported Christians in all generations as they
faced persecutions, famine, and the sword.

Third, the Presence
Is Inescapable

The Presence is everywhere, in everything, before us and
behind us because, of course, that is where God is! Once we
recognize this and understand how the Presence pervades

our lives we can be more responsive to it; as Bernard of Clairvaux, famous French mystic of the twelfth century, so beautifully points out:

Do you awake, well, He, too, is awake.
If you rise in the night-time, if you anticipate to your utmost your earliest awakening,
you will find Him waking you.
You will never anticipate your own awakeness.
In such a relationship, you will be rash if you attribute any priority, any prominent share to yourself;
For He loves both more than you love, and before you love at all.

The Presence is the unseen thrust of the Creator to fashion all Creation to His Will and Plan. We may resist and we may deny, but we only postpone the day when we must cooperate. There is no escape from the subtle power of God, as the writer of Psalm 139 reminds us:

Whither shall I go from thy Spirit?
Or whither shall I flee from thy presence?
If I ascend to heaven, thou art there!
If I make my bed in Sheol, thou art there!
If I take the wings of the morning and dwell in the uttermost parts of the sea,
even there shall thy hand lead me and thy right hand shall hold me.

Fourth, the Presence
Intervenes in Our Lives

The basic belief of a Christian is that God is always seeking to insure that the original purpose of Creation be fulfilled. To do this, God breaks in upon the human scene. He intervened in the history of the Hebrew people, helping them to escape from Egyptian slavery, saving them from the Red Sea, guiding them through the Wilderness, and bringing them to the Promised Land. God also entered human existence through the birth and life and resurrection of Jesus, the Christ. God continues to intervene.

God and the Presence enter life without warning, often entirely unexpectedly; to lift up the brokenhearted, to answer the pleas of the seeker, to redirect the lost, and to convert the sinner. In fact, conversion experiences are recurring examples of the intervention of God.

The best-known illustration is that of *Paul,* which is dramatically reported in the book of Acts. It tells how Paul persecuted Christians. He "entirely approved" of Stephen's death by stoning because Stephen was a Christian. But one day, when on the road to Damascus to arrest more "believers in the Way," Paul had an experience which changed the course of his whole life. A brilliant flash of light struck him to the ground, and he heard the words "Saul, why do you persecute me?" The voice identified itself as coming from Jesus, and directed him to proceed to Damascus where he would find further instructions. When Paul arose, he discovered he could not see; his blindness lasted for three days. When he regained his sight, he was advised by a friend, Ananias, that he had indeed been visited by the Lord and that his mission in life was not to persecute the Christians but to become one of them. From that time on, Paul was a great spokesman for Christ.

St. Augustine is another classic example of the intervention of God. Although he is remembered as one of the most important early theologians of the Christian Church, nevertheless his youth was not known for its spirituality. When he was young he was very attracted to sensual pleasures. Later his intellectual brilliance led him into all sorts of nonreligious explorations. One day as he was walking with a friend, he overheard from a nearby yard the words "Take up and read." He was not sure whether or not the voice came from a child at play, but he finally interpreted it as a message to him from God, and felt that it referred to his Bible, which he had rejected in favor of more intellectual interests. When he returned home, he opened the Book and his eyes fell on the words "Not in rioting or drunkenness, not in strife and envying, but put on the Lord Jesus Christ and make no provision for the flesh" (Romans 13:13).

In telling of the experience later, Augustine wrote: "Instantly at the end of this sentence, by a light as it were of serenity infused into my heart, all the darkness of doubt vanished away."

Although Augustine had already spent years of his life in criticizing the Church, he turned to its beliefs eagerly and energetically. He quickly rose in the ranks and became bishop of Hippo in North Africa. Some of his writings about the Church influence Christians today.

Another example of what appears to be God's intervention occurred on May 24, 1738, to *John Wesley,* while he was an itinerant lay preacher.

In the evening, I went unwillingly to a society in Aldersgate Street, where one was reading Luther's preface to the Epistle to the Romans. About a quarter before nine, while he was describing the change which God works in the heart through faith in Christ, I felt my heart strangely warmed. I felt I did trust in Christ, Christ alone for salvation, and an assurance was given me that He had taken away my sins, even mine, and saved me from the law of sin and death.[1]

The words "I felt my heart strangely warmed" have become well known and oft-repeated whenever folks talk about the religious experiences of John Wesley. Certainly it was an event which changed his life. After it, he was a different person, more sure of his faith and able to speak from firsthand knowledge about the Presence of God.

Evelyn Underhill, a contemporary writer who is considered an authority on matters of the spiritual life, describes the energetic intervention of the Presence as

> an unseen energy other than ourselves, and having, in its own right, a range of being and of significance unconditioned by the narrow human world. We do not mean some immaterial energy, the soul of the evolving universe. We mean a substantial Reality, which is there first in its absolute perfection and living plentitude, which transcends yet penetrates our world, our activity, our souls.[2]

Fifth, the Presence Is
Part of Our Basic Nature

Creation is not just a one-time event. It is a continuing process. God did not just create and then stop on the seventh day. God, through Creation, continually enlarges upon what has been started. Existence is the multiplication of Creation. For example, we can see this in our personal growth. I am more now than when I was born. I continue to create, through new ideas, children, friendships, and more meaningful relationships.

Of course, it is true I can deny God and the Presence by rejecting the movement of Creation. I can destroy life, I can pollute the environment. I can kill the hope of youth or minorities. On the other hand, I can be responsible to the purpose of Creation by seeking to understand my part in it. Meister Eckhart, a notable mystic of the thirteenth century, explains:

> Know that by nature, every creature seeks to become like God. Nature's intent is neither food or drink, nor clothing or comfort, nor anything else in which God is left out. Whether you like it or not, whether you know it or not, secretly nature seeks, hunts, tries to ferret out the track on which God may be found.[3]

It is, therefore, part of my basic nature to be called to "cultivate the Presence" by allowing the Presence to guide my life. In fact, my life will be meaningless if I do not allow it to merge with the overall goal of Creation. This is why Augustine explained, "My soul is restless until it finds rest in Thee."

Every person can have an experience with the Presence. It is part of our divine-human nature. Until each of us has such a relationship, we have not experienced life to its fullest.

The most sublime explanation of the relationship between a person and the Presence of God has been expressed by the writer of Psalm 139:

> O Lord, thou hast searched me and known me.
> Thou knowest when I sit down and when I rise up;
> Thou discernest my thoughts from afar.
> Thou searchest out my path and my lying down,
> And art acquainted with all my ways.

God is a part of us and we are a part of God, separate but eternally wedded. It is God in whom "we live and move and have our being." Certainly God, through the Presence, is part of our basic nature.

Sixth, The Presence Calls Us
to Consider Others More Than Self

In the biographies of many who have been touched by the Presence, we discover that they not only live lives of prayer and meditation but also give of themselves, without counting the cost, to vocations of healing the sick, teaching the uneducated, and visiting the imprisoned. Indeed, many have written inspiring devotional books while at the same time being engrossed in building hospitals, founding schools, and alleviating hunger.

The visitation of the Presence is a mind-expanding event. The original self-centeredness of human nature is broken open to a new awareness of the world.

There is a legend concerning the mother of St. Peter. Her life had not been a very memorable one, so, when she died, she found herself in the horribleness of hell. Her son kept asking her if there was not some good act she had done which would earn her release, but she could not think of any. Finally, after much reflection, she remembered that she had once given an onion to a hungry beggar. Immediately a giant onion appeared and descended from heaven. With excitement and much thanksgiving, she grasped the vegetable and was being drawn upward slowly when others saw that she was escaping. They quickly grabbed her legs. As the mother of St. Peter rose in the air, she shook herself free from the added burdens, dropping those who were holding onto her into the smoking pit. But even as she shook, the outer skin of the onion peeled away and she, too, fell back with the others. And so it went. Each time she grasped the onion and began to rise, the others sought her aid in their own escape. Each time she selfishly shook them off, the skin peeled away again. Finally, when she was willing to pull the others to safety, the onion did not break apart. All entered heaven because she gave of herself that they could enter with her.

Persons of the Presence discover the truth of this story very early in their pilgrimage toward God. The original sin of being concerned only with self gives way to the greater awareness of the needs of others.

Notes

1. John Wesley, *Journal,* ed. P. L. Parker (Chicago: Moody, 1974), p. 64.
2. Evelyn Underhill, *The Mystic Way,* 1913 (New York: Dutton reprint).
3. Meister Eckhart, *Meister Eckhart,* tr. Raymond Blakney (New York: Harper & Bros., 1957).

2

METHODS OF CULTIVATING THE PRESENCE

There is no single method to follow. Some well-known leaders have used a particular style, while other persons, equally important, have been successful with different approaches.

For example, in the fourth century, St. Augustine cultivated the Presence through the use of *intellectual search*. He had a brilliant mind. He had much experience as a teacher. He was used to the academic processes of reasoning and debate. Hence he expressed his experience with the Presence in intellectual fashion.

Ignatius Loyola, in the fourteenth century, established a lasting religious order (the Jesuits) on the *strict structure of spiritual exercises*. Loyola had spent some years in the army and he knew the importance of regulations and authority. Hence, his expression of the cultivation process was formed on the pattern of orders and disciplines.

On the other hand, John Woolman, the Quaker leader of the eighteenth century, achieved his great sense of the spiritual life without the employment of either intellectual search or strict disciplines. He experienced the Presence *without following any set plan at all*. He rejected set prayers or long reasonings in favor of being guided by the Inner Light of the Quaker belief. It enabled him to experience the Presence as he worked in his tailor shop, spoke at Quaker meetings, or dealt with the Indians.

So the cultivation of the Presence is not dependent upon any one procedure. Each of us must choose the method which seems best suited to our individual nature. "Never forget," wrote Baron von Hügel, the Catholic counselor on spiritual matters in this twentieth century, "the enormous variety of souls."

Although each person's experience with the Presence

may be different, there are seven basic steps which seekers have found rewarding. (a) Deciding How to Begin; (b) Deciding How to Spend Your Time; (c) Free-Style Cultivation; (d) The Use of Disciplines; (e) The Practice of Prayer; (f) About Special Readings; (g) The Rewards of Silence.

Deciding How to Begin

First, begin where you are. In 1912, as she was beginning her successful spiritual journey (which led her to become the author of more books on the spiritual life than any other recent British author), Evelyn Underhill wrote to Baron von Hügel, asking how she should begin. In reply, von Hügel, an experienced "director of souls," wrote:

> Simply feed your soul on the great positive facts and truths you see already. Pray for fidelity to your light as may be within God's plan for you. And as for the rest, neither force adhesion nor allow rejection, but let it alone, as possible food for others and indeed for yourself later on. It does not concern yourself at present.[1]

Later he cautioned that she should not be concerned about the procedure.

> We must always in our efforts strive to reach what we have not got by the faithful practice of what we have. Although God is no way tied in His dealings with us as to the procedure.[2]

Von Hügel was saying that we should take the step which appears before us and not worry about the future. After all,

God cannot be commanded or programmed. We may experience His Presence in even the simplest methods that we follow.

In the beginning, establish a place for cultivation. Although it is important to be willing to "start where you are," it is also true that some definite guidelines must be set so that you may develop a sense of continuity. For example, William Law, who wrote *A Serious Call to a Devout and Holy Life,* which has been a devotional guide since 1728, says:

> If you were to use yourself (as far as you can) to pray always in the same place; if you were to reserve that place for devotion, and not allow yourself to do anything common in it; if you were never to be there yourself, but in times of devotion; if any room, or (if that cannot be) if any particular part of a room was thus used, this kind of consecration of it as a place holy unto God, would have an effect upon your mind, and dispose you to such tempers, as would very much assist your devotion.[3]

In some parts of the world, such as India, members of a family will ask to be temporarily released from the family chores in order to withdraw to some secluded place for spiritual renewal. Americans could well follow such a means of keeping the Spirit alive. While riding a commuter train, why not close your eyes for moments of meditation instead of reading about the latest murder. When your lunch break comes, a few moments in prayer will not only make the sandwiches taste better but will make a difference in your response to the conversation of others. A few moments of meditation before the children come home from school, or a habitual prayer just before entering the office of a customer, will bring a change in your life and the response of others. Any place, repeatedly used for prayer, becomes a reminder that when there, it is time for meditation. The results will amaze you.

Follow a simple plan to help you along. Sooner or later, you will want to adopt some plan to follow. It does not have to be complicated or elaborate. Even the simplest method is enough to get you started.

One of the least involved procedures is suggested by the Quaker Thomas Kelly. (Kelly was a war-relief worker in Europe in 1917. Later he taught at Haverford College. He is perhaps best remembered for *A Testament of Devotion,* a book on the life of the Spirit.) He suggests four different steps: (1) Have a vision, an objective, a goal and dream. Decide what you wish would happen. (2) Start where you are at present, as von Hügel suggests. Begin now. Start today. (3) Do not worry if you stumble and fall. Just pick yourself up and start again. Self-accusations are not necessary or helpful. (4) Getting uptight is destructive. Continue your efforts in a relaxed frame of mind.

> [1.] The first step to . . . obedience . . . is the flaming vision of the wonder of such a life, a vision which comes occasionally to us all. . . .

> [2.] Once having the vision, the second step to holy obedience is this: Begin where you are. Obey now. Use what little obedience you are capable of, even if it be like a grain of mustard seed. Begin where you are. Live this present moment, this present hour as you sit in your seats, in utter, utter submission and openness toward Him. Listen outwardly to these words, but within, behind

the scenes, in the deeper levels of your lives where you are all alone with God, the Loving Eternal One, keep up a silent prayer.

[3.] And the third step in holy obedience . . . is this: If you slip and stumble and forget God for an hour, and assert your old proud self, and rely upon your own clever wisdom, don't spend too much time in anguished regrets and self-accusations but begin again, just where you are.

[4.] Yet a fourth consideration in holy obedience is this: Don't grit your teeth and clench your fists and say, "I will! I will!" Relax. Take hands off. Submit yourself to God. Learn to live in the passive voice . . . and let life be willed through you. For "I will" spells not obedience"[4]

As you cultivate the Presence, find someone to act as your spiritual guide. The guidance of a seasoned "spiritual director" is as important to the spiritual journey as the map is to the vacationer. Roman Catholic persons have long since become aware of this through the Church's traditional teaching about retreats. On the other hand, Protestants need a special reminder about the role of the spiritual guide, which can be either a person or a book.

One of the Roman Catholic writers who speaks from much experience about the need for a spiritual director is Thomas Merton. Having had twenty-seven years of training in contemplation and monastic life, Merton wrote often about religious growth. In his book *Spiritual Direction and Meditation,* he stresses the importance of the counselor:

Nevertheless human nature is weak, and the kindly support and wise advice of one whom we trust often enables us to accept more perfectly what we already know and see in an obscure way. A director may not tell us anything we do not already know, but it is a great thing if he helps us to overcome our hesitations. . . . However, in many cases, a director will reveal to us things which we have hitherto been unable to see, though they were staring us in the face.[5]

Francis de Sales, who was canonized by the Church in 1665 after a cleric's life of working for the poor, as well as significant writing (he wrote *Introduction to a Devout Life*), also speaks out strongly about the wisdom of having a guide:

> The young Tobias, when commanded to go to Rages, said:
> "I have no knowledge of the way."
> "Go then," replied his father, "and seek out some man to guide thee."
> I say the same to you, Philothea. Do you wish, in good earnest, to set on the way to devotion? Seek out some good man to guide and conduct you; it is the admonition of admonitions.[6]

Deciding How to Spend Your Time

The second step involves learning how to use your time. You and I have just a limited amount of it. We have attractions and responsibilities on every side. The needs of our families, our jobs, our neighborhood, our recreation, our health—all these compete with our need for time of religious development.

In order not to become like people blown to and fro by every wind of circumstance, we need to save some of our time for personal prayer, regular devotional reading, quiet meditation and thinking about the purpose and direction of our lives.

William Law writes about the importance of time in his book *A Serious Call to a Devout and Holy Life,* which he wrote in England in a period when people needed spiritual awakening:

> A quarter hour of prayer brings you out of your closet a new man, your heart feels the good of it; and every return of such a prayer gives new life and new growth to all your virtues with more certainty than the dew refreshes the herbs of the field.[7]

A spiritual guide of the seventeenth century, Jeremy Taylor (who gave practical advice on *Holy Living* and *Holy Dying* to the people of his day), reminds us of how much we get for our few moments of spiritual investment:

> And, indeed, if we consider how much of our lives is taken up with the needs of nature; how many years are wholly spent, before we come to any use of reason; how many years more, before that reason is useful to us to any great purposes; how imperfect our discourse is made by our evil education, false principles, ill company, bad examples and want of experience; how many parts of our wisest and best years are spent in eating and sleeping, in necessary businesses and unnecessary vanities, in worldly civilities and less useful circumstances, in the learning arts and sciences, languages and trades; that little portion of hours that is left for the practice of piety and walking with God, is so short and trifling, that were not the goodness of God infinitely great, it might seem unreasonable or impossible for us to expect of Him eternal joys in heaven even after well spending those few minutes which are left for God and God's service, after we have served ourselves and our own occasions.[8]

How much time should be given to religious growth? Different people need different answers to that question but a suggestion from Baron von Hügel seems appropriate in most instances. Answering a letter of inquiry from Evelyn Underhill, he wrote:

> I dare not say that I would only restrict you to only one quarter of an hour a day. You might find two such helpful. But I would not encourage more than fifteen minutes at any one time, else you sink into just ordinary reading.[9]

When she sought his counsel a second time, twelve years after the first, von Hügel suggested:

Deliberate prayer . . . one-fourth to one-half hour a day.

Three to five minutes' examination of conscience before sleep.

One religious retreat a year, without membership in any particular religious group.

Cultivation of some nonreligious interest such as music or gardening.

Two afternoons a week visiting the poor.

> I believe you ought to get yourself gently and gradually interested in the poor. That you should visit them, very quietly and unostentatiously, with as little incorporation as possible into Visiting Societies.[10]

It is miraculous how the measurement of time changes when it is applied to the inner life of the Spirit. One moment or two of true confession can relieve a heart heavily burdened with months of guilt. Just five minutes of sincere prayer has been known to cleanse a soul of years of sinful living. A whole lifetime of meaninglessness can be erased by one genuine appeal for pardon, such as happened to the robber who confessed and was pardoned, as he hung on the cross beside Christ.

In the matter of time, then, the believing person has a tremendous advantage. But I must warn against expecting quick results even from the most fervent pleas. The forgiveness of God may be freely given, but it is not cheaply given. Forgiveness may be instantaneous, as it was for the robber on the cross beside Christ, but it is not cheap.

It is important to make this point lest the beginner conclude that forgiveness can be purchased with small amounts of prayer. In our society we are used to instant gratification. But in the majority of situations, rewards in the spiritual life are long in coming. Although small satisfactions begin to appear immediately, greater returns come only to those who have invested deeply in the spiritual life.

"O Lord, this is not the work of one day, nor children's sport," observed Thomas à Kempis, the probable author of *Imitation of Christ,* a book which is next to the Bible in devotional popularity.

Free-Style Cultivation

If you have decided how you want to begin and how much time you want to invest, what is the next decision about cultivating the Presence? At this point the seeker has to decide between alternate choices. He or she can (1) *proceed without any set program,* letting the Spirit blow where it will, waiting upon the Presence and following Its guidance, or (2) *establish a pattern* of regular and disciplined readings, prayers, and exercises.

The choice between these two procedures faces all who

begin this journey. Each way has its champions. Each way has proven to be helpful. Your choice should be based on your personal habits.

Are you a carefree person? Do you accomplish your goals without too much scheduling? Can you establish a distant goal and stick to it without constant checkups and reminders? If so, you might choose the first procedure.

If you are a meticulous planner, if you enjoy following a schedule, if you work best under discipline, if you find regular habits necessary to keep you on target, then the second plan might be best for you.

First we will deal with those who prefer the free-style method of spiritual cultivation.

Those who advocate the free-style method point out that cultivation of the Spirit is more a matter of *intent* than of *form*. It is more a matter of *desire* than of *method*. They suggest that if you wish, you can find time to pray on the train, while waiting for a traffic light, or sitting in the waiting room of any office. Each of these times offers the opportunity to ask the Will of God for the next thing that you should do. A prayer moment can change the day from purposelessness to meaningfulness.

One of the best-known exponents of the undisciplined method is Brother Lawrence, otherwise known as Nicholas Herman, whom I mentioned earlier.

Along with his work in the monastery kitchen, he revealed a great sense of the Presence. He prayed while washing pots and pans. He cultivated the Spirit while peeling potatoes. He found time to meditate on the meaning of Creation while looking out the scullery window. He prayed at no set times but, rather, at all times: cooking, serving, washing up.

Having found in many books different methods of going to God, and divers practices of the spiritual life, I thought this would rather puzzle me than facilitate what I sought after, which was nothing but how to become wholly God's. This made me resolve to give the all for the all; so, after having given myself wholly to God, I began to live as if there was no one but He and I in the world."[11]

Brother Lawrence even rebelled against the rigorous orders of worship of the established Church.

I have quitted all forms of devotion and set prayers, save those which my state obligates me. And I make it my only business to persevere in His holy presence, wherein I keep myself by a simple attention and absorbing passionate regard to God."[12]

The Presence is not a product of *design*. It is a product of *motive*. Indeed, Dietrich Bonhoeffer, Christian martyr of the twentieth century, puts it well when he says:

There is nothing of religious method here. The "religious act" is always something partial; "faith" is something whole, involving the whole of one's life. Jesus calls men, not to a new religion, but to life.

Our relation to God is not a "religious" relationship . . . but a new life in "existence for others."[13]

The Use of Disciplines

While some people find free-style methods more valuable, others prefer the use of planned disciplines. Over the past centuries, those who believe that the journey to spiritual achievement can be made only through the employment of established exercises have argued forcefully for their position. John Baillie, a modern English theologian, is one of these and explains the position:

> The culture of the spiritual life requires a strict discipline. You and I must be ruthless with ourselves, if the light of knowledge of the Glory of God is to survive within us. Jesus said that though ''the light of the eye is the light of the body'' yet ''if thy right eye offend thee, pluck it out and cast it from thee.''
>
> And now, last, we cannot be in any doubt as to the kind of spiritual discipline to which we should subject ourselves. It has all been worked out through long ages by the prophets and the apostles, by the saints and the martyrs.
>
> My own experience has been that there are some enjoyments, some distractions, some ways of spending my time, from which I must firmly turn aside, if I am going to keep the Spirit alive within me. I can say nothing against them in the abstract; they may be innocent enough in themselves, they may even be all right for other people, but I know myself well enough to be sure that I cannot afford to indulge in them without danger of losing the Pearl of Great Price.
>
> They are like the weeds in our gardens. There is nothing wrong with the weeds themselves. Each of them has its own humble, honorable place among the flora. But we dare not let them grow where they are, lest they choke the tender plants which the garden is intended to nurture.[14]

It is interesting to observe the differences yet similarities between disciplines.

1. Evelyn Underhill, who knows whereof she speaks as a prolific writer on the spiritual life, says we should proceed along the lines of five steps:

Awakening
Discipline
Enlightenment
Self-surrender
Union

2. Another generalized process would be as follows:

1. Adoration: We become aware of the wonder and mystery of life. We meet a better person than we are. We discover beauty and truth.
2. Confession: We know we are not what we ought to be. We admit our dark side. Our sins separate us from others.
3. Petition: We would like to change. We cannot do it by ourselves. We reach out for guidance.
4. Intercession: We discover there is help. The unseen response to prayer and request brings a change in us. The Presence is intervening.
5. Thanksgiving: We appreciate the new life. We give thanks for change.
6. Commitment: We feel the need to become more of a part of others. Living by or for ourselves is lonely. We want to give our lives to someone.

3. Another overall view of discipline is found in the *Theologica Germanica,* which suggests these three fundamental steps to experiencing the Presence: (1) purification, (2) enlightenment, and (3) union. The author, whose name we do not know, puts the matter this way:

No one can be enlightened unless he be first cleansed or purified and stripped. So also, no one can be united with God unless he first be enlightened. Thus there are three stages: first, the purification (or purgation); second, the enlightening; third, the union.[15]

4. Another sample of discipline is that of Jan Ruys-broeck, who was one of the influential mystics to come out of the Netherlands in the Middle Ages. He is still looked upon as a sound reference because of his ability to combine the inner life of the Spirit with the outer life of social con-sciousness. Ruysbroeck established an Order which lasted for many years on what he called *The Seven Steps of the Ladder of Spiritual Love*. If you followed the rungs, he said, you would be able to climb into the Presence of God.

First: Conformity with the Will of God.
Second: Voluntary poverty and renunciation of possessions.
Third: Purity and a chaste life.
Fourth: Humbleness.
Fifth: Unselfish love and honor of God.
Sixth: Following the contemplative life.
Seventh: Complete absorption in God.

5. Below you will find an outline of the method for spiritual growth suggested by Jean Nicholas Grou, in the eighteenth century. He was a monk with the Society of Jesus in France. He wrote a good deal about matters of the interior life, and his *Manual for Interior Souls* has been translated into many languages. In it, he outlines this plan for spiritual development:

1. The first step is *to have the desire* to attain inner peace; to acknowledge that it takes effort and determination.
2. The second step is to *plan how we are going to proceed* with our desire. We must take account of our age, health, and state of life as we choose that plan which we agree to faithfully follow.
3. We must always *remember that God is present* to guide us, and to forgive us when we fail.

4. Then we must be willing to *set aside the time necessary* to do the necessary praying and meditating.
5. The fifth step is to *make confession* of those things of which we find ourselves accused in our prayers and meditations.
6. It is important to *choose our spiritual reading* with care.
7. The seventh step involves *becoming more able to discipline our Selves.* At this point, Grou observes "that everything within us draws us toward the slavery of the senses and self-love. We must struggle continually against our inclinations. . . . This is painful in the beginning but it becomes easy as we grow accustomed to retiring into ourselves and keeping ourselves in the presence of God."
8. The eighth step, according to Grou, a Roman Catholic, is to *seek the help of the Blessed Virgin.* Persons of different religious persuasions may prefer to turn to their "Guardian Angel" or their "Presence of God."
9. Finally, Grou recommends *having a good spiritual guide,* which, we conclude, might be a spiritual director of souls or, lacking this, an authentic spiritual guidebook.

As can be seen immediately from this outline of spiritual progress, the effort is not complicated. Nor is it unusual. Nor is it peculiar to any one generation or life-style. The Presence never hides behind complexity. It can be cultivated by every person.

The Practice of Prayer

Every Person Prays Sometime

Prayer is the fifth method you may use to cultivate the Presence.

Almost everyone has prayed, especially during times of crisis. William Shakespeare reflected this human instinct in the opening scene of his play *The Tempest* when, in the midst of a violent storm at sea, the fearful sailors cry out: "All lost! to prayers, to prayers! all lost!"

Indeed, everyone seems to have a need for the Divine, as St. Augustine testifies in his famous sentence, "I am restless until I find my rest in Thee." Some people even suggest that a person is a "praying animal."

There are occasions when practically everyone finds that human frailty, combined with difficult circumstances, forces him or her to cry out desperately for help. Even agnostics and atheists express this deep need at times.

It is not a sign of weakness to pray but, rather, an acknowledgment that we are finite beings in an infinite world and we need more understanding and strength.

How Often Should We Pray?

Paul advocated that a person should "pray without ceasing." Martin Luther, also, urges constant prayer for all Christians. In "Table Talk" he says:

> Therefore, where there is a Christian, there is also the Holy Spirit, and he does nothing else save pray continually. For even if the mouth be not always moving and uttering words, yet the heart goes on beating unceasingly with cries like these, "Ah, dear Father, may Thy name be hallowed, may Thy kingdom come, and Thy Will be done." And whenever there comes sore buffetings and trials, then the aspiration and supplication increase, even audibly, so that you cannot find a Christian man who does not pray; just as you cannot find a living man without a pulse that never stands still. . . .[16]

One of the insights which come to those who pray is the ability to pray and still be a part of the daily activity of the world. Even in the midst of the pressures of each day, the pray-er finds it possible to continue the inner security of prayer. Thomas Kelly, the Quaker, tells us how this can be practiced and accomplished:

> Walk on the streets. Chat with your friends. But every moment, behind the scenes, be in prayer, offering yourself in complete obedience. I find this internal continuous prayer-life absolutely essential. It can be carried on day and night, in the thick of business, in home or school. Such prayer of submission can be so simple. It is well to use a single sentence, repeated over and over, such as this: "Be Thou my will." ... "Be Thou my will."
>
> This hidden prayer-life can pass, in time, beyond words and phrases into mere ejaculations, "My God."
>
> Words may cease and one stands and walks and sits and lies in wordless attitudes of adoration and submission and rejoicing and glory.[17]

The Importance of Prayer

If prayer is a universal characteristic of all persons, then we ought to give it a higher priority in life than most of us do. William Law, about whom we have spoken before, urges this upon every person:

> He who has learned to pray has learned the greatest secret of a happy and holy life. Which way soever we lose our hearts, they will return to us again empty. Time will convince the vainest minds that happiness is no more to be found in the things of this world than it is to be dug out of the earth. But when the motions of our hearts are motions

tending to God . . . then it is that we have found out a good suited to our natures that is equal to our wants. For he that lives in the spirit of devotion, lives at the top of human happiness, and is the farthest removed from all vanities and vexations which disturb and weary the minds of men who are devoted to the world.[18]

Prayer Is Not Just Talking to Ourselves

Those who demean or criticize prayer claim that it is nothing more than talking to oneself. Even if that were true, prayer would be helpful. Most of us need to give more thought to the purpose and direction of our lives. "Know thyself" is a basic admonition found in many religions. If prayer can deepen this process, then it is worthwhile. A better knowledge of who we are and what we are living for is the beginning of growth of the spirit. Once people become accustomed to reflection, they begin to get even deeper benefits from prayer. St. Teresa, who is remembered because of her life spent in reforming the convent structure of the Church of Spain, advises:

> We must not content ourselves with liberty and gusts in prayer. We must come out from prayer the most sweet, only to do harder and harder works for God and our neighbors. Otherwise the prayer is not good, and the gusts are not from God. For my part, and I have been long at it, I desire no other gift from prayer but that which ends in every day making me a better and better woman.[19]

Prayer and Personal Discipline

The different postures in which prayer is pursued are symbolic reminders of the variety of ways by which prayer can be practiced. Moses and Job said their prayers while sitting. Hezekiah lay on his bed. King David often prayed while walking. Abraham prayed while lying face down upon the floor. The tax-gatherer stood all alone to pray. And Paul wrote that "for this reason, I bow my knees." Certainly there is no one form or discipline for the practice of prayer.

The clue to successful praying lies more in the motive than in the method. A genuine desire to obtain the benefits of prayer will carry the beginner through early failures, no matter what method is used. Brother Lawrence, whom we mentioned earlier, used no method at all. He explains one of the secrets of his prayer life:

> When the mind, for lack of discipline, when first we engage in devotion, has contracted bad habits of wandering and dissipation, such habits are difficult to overcome, and commonly draw us, even against our will, to things on earth.

> I believe that one remedy for this is to confess our faults, and to humble ourselves before God. I do not advise you to use multiplicity of words in prayer; discursive forms are often the occasion of wandering. Hold yourself in prayer before God, like a poor, dumb, paralytic beggar at the rich man's gate. Let it be your business to keep your mind on the Presence of the Lord. . . . if you persevere with your whole strength, God will have pity on you.[20]

So, pray . . . just pray . . . the words don't matter . . . the form is not important . . . let the desire express your feeling in any form . . . keep at it without stopping. You will find the prayer style that fulfills your need.

When Should a Person Pray?

If the prayer life of Jesus of Nazareth can be used as an example here, then the time to pray is before the difficult periods of life. Jesus seems to have resorted to prayer just before His most critical experiences. He faced the Temptation with a background of prayer. He went aside and prayed before the Arrest. He prayed before the Trial. He prayed before the Crucifixion, and He prayed at the moment of His Death. Prayer can be, therefore, a preparation for future events.

I do not mean to imply that prayer "prays away" the future. Not at all. We have to live with the consequences of our past actions. Even Jesus suffered because His faithfulness in the past antagonized those who disliked Him. I mean prayer prepares us for the responsibilities of the future. A few moments of prayer can fortify a soul to face trouble or trial. As the psalmist affirmed in his prayer: "Thou art my rock," I shall not be moved (Psalm 31:3).

I cannot overemphasize the significance of praying out of the depths of our lives. The important part of prayer is to get our inner feelings out honestly, to be as straightforward as we can be, with our own human nature and all its divinity and frailty. François Fénelon, a spiritual adviser to the immoral court of Louis XIV of France, knew a great deal about human weakness. But Fénelon kept his own integrity. His counsel is a model for us all:

> Tell God all that is in your heart, as one unloads one's heart,
> its pleasures and its pains, to a friend.
>
> Tell Him your troubles, that He may comfort you;
> Tell Him your joys, that He may sober them;

Tell Him your longings, that He may purify them;
Tell Him your dislikes, that He may help you conquer them;
Talk to Him of your temptations, that He may shield you;
Show Him the wounds on your heart, that He may heal
    them;

Lay bare your indifference to good,
    your depraved tastes for evil,
    your instability.

Tell Him how self-love makes you unjust to others,
    how vanity tempts you to be insecure,
    how pride disguises you to yourself as to others.

If you thus pour out all of your weaknesses, needs, troubles, there will be no lack of what to say. You will never exhaust the subject. It is continually being renewed. People who have no secrets from each other never want for subjects of conversation. They do not weigh their words, for there is nothing to be held back; neither do they seek for something to say. They talk out of the abundance of the heart without consideration, just what they think. Blessed are they who attain to such familiar unreserved intercourse with God.[21]

Concerning the "Dry" Periods

No matter how deeply we long to feel close to the Presence, one of the most common obstacles to a rewarding prayer experience is the "dry" period. This is the time when there is no desire at all to pray. We wonder why we ever thought it was important. Such a time comes to even the most experienced pray-ers. It seems to come unannounced and often without explanation. Periods of spiritual drought affect even the most faithful, as St. Teresa, famous for her faith, admitted:

At times I find myself so arid that I am not able to form any distinct image of God, nor can I put my soul into any attitude of prayer. My mind at such times is like a born fool. . . . What would those who loved and honour me think if they saw their friend in this dotage?[22]

Another person who was far advanced in the habit of prayer, Baron von Hügel, also admits to the experience of dryness:

Spiritual dryness is inevitable in the life of prayer. We will be much helped to bear these desert stretches, by recognition of the normality and the necessity of such desolation. We will thus come to true desolation in religion as we treat the recurrence of the night within every twenty-four hours of our physical existence, or as the body wearies at the end of any protracted exertion in our physical life.

When desolation is upon us, we will quietly modify the kind and amount of our prayer. . . .[23]

There are several answers to these unproductive periods. One is to make sure, in the very beginning, that you observe a definite pattern for praying; set aside special times—in the morning upon arising, or in the evening—and a special place. If you have established the habit well, you will find that you may continue to "pray through" the dry periods.

A more complete response to dry periods is to reflect that they are only temporary at best, as von Hügel reminded his niece in several memorable illustrations which had been suggested to him by his own spiritual adviser, Father Raymond Hocking. For instance, if you were going on a sea voyage, you would know before you even left port that at some point the seas would become rough. Therefore, it would be wise upon embarking to make sure that the trunk in your cabin would be secure and that all your belongings or gear would not slide all over the deck. Then when the dirty weather came, you could wait it out and after it had passed, engage in your usual pursuits once again.

Von Hügel remembered Father Hocking telling him another helpful story: You might be going on a journey across the desert. Even as you mounted the camel for a strange ride, you would know that sooner or later the wind would blow up a sandstorm. When it came there would be nothing to do but "dismount from the camel, fall prostrate face downwards on the sand, covering your head with your cloak, and lie, thus for an hour, three hours, half a day: the sandstorm will go, and you will arise, as if nothing had happened."[24]

There is no use fighting the dry times that come, with a certain naturalness, into the life of all pray-ers. Perhaps they have a function of enforcing a period of rest in the spiritual pilgrimage or providing a time for perspective on the journey. Whatever their reason, it is best just to wait them out and then when they are over, as with the storms at sea or on the desert, resume your voyage again "as if nothing had happened."

For What Should We Pray?

It is necessary to realize that one of the reasons why prayer does not "produce results" lies in the objectives for which we pray, not in the act of praying. For example, if I wish to stop overeating, I should not pray that I might not stuff myself with food. Rather, I should pray that I would become thin. It is important not to stress the malady but to emphasize the cure. Pray forward, not backward. Pray up, not down. Pray positively, not negatively. It does no good to reiterate our failures. Rather, let us pray for our objectives.

The apostle Paul knew well of the frailty of human nature and how persons such as you and I tend to weakness. But rather than reminding us of our failures, he wrote we should concentrate on "whatsoever is pure, whatsoever is of good report . . . think on these things." Von Hügel, too, warns us against praying about evil, when we should be praying about the possible good:

> We let our imagination and sensitiveness be directly absorbed in our trouble. We contemplate, and further enlarge the trouble present in ourselves; instead of firmly and faithfully looking away, either at the great abiding realities of the spiritual world, or at some wholesome fact or law.
>
> The error lies in our lurking suspicions that, for such trials to purify us, we must face them directly. It ignores the experience of God's saints across the ages, that, precisely in proportion as we get away from direct occupation with our troubles, do and will these trials purify our souls.[25]

Interpreting the Answers to Prayer

Although praying seems to be a simple matter, the fact is that it is an extremely complicated expression of the mind and heart.

So often we pray only for an immediate need, praying for the fulfillment of something very much on our minds. We tend to overlook the long-term aspects of our petition. For example, the child prays that his father give him a bicycle. However, the father knows that it is too early in the child's life for him to have a bicycle so does not grant the request. It would be wrong for the child to become angry. The parent was really answering the prayer to the very best interests of the child.

So it often is with our prayers. We pray for needs, the granting of which, as *we* want, would not be good.

Paul may have had this understanding in mind when he wrote to the Romans: ''we do not know how to pray as we ought.''

Thus prayers that appear to be unanswered may (in reality) be answered very well. If we think we are not getting results from our prayers, we should look again.

Too often we pray with the idea of ''my will be done.'' We need to remember that we are part of a larger fabric of life. Instead of praying for relief from an affliction, it may be more important to pray for strength to accept and overcome the trouble. Then we will have grown in courage and patience and wisdom.

Long ago St. Francis put this insight into poetry:

I asked God for strength, that I might achieve;
   I was made weak, that I might learn to obey.
I asked for health, that I might do great things;
   I was given infirmity, that I might do better things.

I asked for riches, that I might be happy;
   I was given poverty, that I might be wise.
I asked for power, that I might have the praise of men;
   I was given weakness, that I might feel the need of God.

I asked for all things, that I might enjoy life;
   I was given life, that I might enjoy all things.

I received nothing that I had asked for—
   Everything I had hoped for.
My prayers were answered.[26]

About Special Readings

The sixth method for cultivating the Presence is to employ books which are of a special type. They are sometimes referred to as books of "devotions." They are different from any other kind of literature.

For example, while reading books on history or biography, our minds are often critical, analytical, and sometimes argumentative. But in devotional reading, our whole being, not just our intellect, is involved. We read to fulfill the whole inner person.

The best devotional book is the book of Psalms. It is to be read with an open heart and rarely, if ever, with a mind bent on analysis, criticism or argument. It has a message for the whole Spirit. It is a companion for the soul.

Other examples of excellent devotional reading are: *Imitation of Christ* by Thomas à Kempis; *Private Devotions* by Lancelot Andrewes; *Christian Perfection* by François Fénelon; *Rule and Exercises of Holy Living* by Jeremy Taylor; *A Serious Call to a Devout and Holy Life* by William Law; *Pilgrim's Progress* by John Bunyan.

Devotional reading is not educational, in which the reader gains more facts. It is not historical, in which past events are described. It is not like reading a novel, in which characters work out some plot. Nor is it cheaply inspirational; it should not tell you how to overcome your problems in easy lessons or how to pray for the things you think you need. Instead, devotional reading reflects the movement of the Spirit, as Thomas Merton suggests:

> Reflection does not refer to a purely intellectual activity, and still less does it refer to mere reasoning. Reflection

involves not only the mind but also the heart, and indeed our whole being. One who really meditates does not merely think, he also loves. . . .[27]

Another characteristic of devotional literature is that it does not contain arguments in favor of the spiritual life any more than the Bible argues for the existence of God. Devotional books, like the Bible, assume the presence of God.

Devotional books seek, rather, to enlighten the Spirit than to educate the mind. They are not books *about* God as much as they are *of* God; not *about* the spiritual life but *of* that life. They are not as interested in academic discussion or debate as they are in revealing the Spirit. They are not written to express an opinion but to speak for a Presence.

Devotional books should be read differently from other books. They should be read with an attitude of meditation. In discussing how to read the Psalms, Merton points out:

> However this penetration of the meaning of the Psalms was not just a matter of studying them with the aid of a commentary. It was a question of "savoring" and "absorbing" the meaning of the Psalms in the depths of one's own heart . . . so that the Psalms gradually come to be as intimate and personal as one's own reflections and feelings. Thus the Psalms "form" the mind and heart according to the mind and heart of Christ.[28]

Meditative reading, therefore, is not so much an achievement as an experience. Just as no passing glance at a great painting will ever suffice to reveal the secret of its composition, so no speed-reading of a devotional classic will ever really be rewarding. The painting or the book must be allowed to "have its way with us." *They* become the active agents, not *we*. A devotional classic must be read and reread any number of times before its real power begins to claim us.

Douglas Steere, an American Quaker, who writes extensively on the devotional classics, and who has combined a lifetime interest in retreats, religious workcamps, and devotional writing, sums up the value of devotional reading in the following manner:

> In reading devotional literature, the limitations of time, and the wisdom of those who have used it most profitably, agree in urging the wise use of the veto. We cannot read all. You must select. Find a few spiritual "staples" and feed on them until you know them. Be proud to be ignorant of vast areas of the "religious book" field. Nowhere does novelty count so little as in devotional reading. Few young people today, and too few of those in my generation, have ever carefully read the same book through five times or even three. A real devotional book is one that you can live with year after year and that never stales or never fails to speak to some needs in your life.[29]

The Rewards of Silence

The seventh method for the cultivation of the Presence is the use of silence. It is a technique that is as old as the psalms: "Be still and know that I am God"; or as old as the ancient prophet Isaiah, who urged people to "wait upon the Lord" in order to "renew their strength." Still later in Scripture, Jesus found the use of silence rewarding, for he often withdrew from the crowds to some solitary place.

Silence opens the mind to new understandings. It allows

the creative spirit of the Presence to enter the heart. It sweeps away much of the disorganizing influence of too much anxious activity. It allows the mind to find its own depths. It enables us to get in touch with our real selves. Silence helps the inner life express itself more freely. It gives us the opportunity to sort out our feelings, emotions, and inner values. Indeed, many devotional books about the spirit urge us to practice silence, as does *Imitation of Christ:*

> In silence and in stillness, the religious soul grows and learns the mysteries of Holy Writ. . . . whosoever, therefore, draws himself from his acquaintances and friends, God will draw near unto him . . . . shut the door behind thee, and call unto thee, Jesus thy Beloved. Stay with him in the cell; for thou shalt not find so great peace elsewhere.[30]

Silence means many things. It can be like sitting in a small boat in the middle of a calm lake on a hot summer afternoon. It can be like the eerie quietness of the forest before a violent storm. It can be the freighted silence of an angry spouse. It can be the enjoyment of a fulfilled passion. Real silence is more than any of these. It is a complete emptiness of the soul, as the following story suggests:

> An active and energetic American once journeyed to a monastery in the Egyptian desert. "I have heard," he told the monks, "that you have found inner peace and joy. I have come to learn the secret for myself!"
>
> "Then, go into the desert," they directed, "and be silent."
>
> After a while the visitor returned and was asked if he had found silence. "Of course," he replied. "I heard no voice among the sands."
>
> "What did you think about?" the monks asked.

"O, a thousand things passed through my mind."

"Then you did not find silence. Go back and become quiet. Let your aloneness comfort your anxious soul. When you find silence, you will find peace and joy."

At first glance this emphasis upon inner emptiness may seem unreasonable. When people seek more meaning to life they usually conclude they should increase their number of friends, social interests, and educational knowledge. But there are those who feel that such efforts may really drain our spiritual selves and separate us from a better knowledge of our own real identities. One person who believed this and wrote about it with persuasion was the unknown author of *The Cloud of Unknowing,* a book of counsel about how to find complete emptiness, written in the fourteenth century. It suggested that in order to experience creative silence, we must empty our minds of all ideas, plans, feelings, impressions, and even memories. Only the cloud of knowing nothing opens the soul to the invasion of the Presence. Inasmuch as God cannot be apprehended by our intellect, we have to be accepting in the spirit. This thesis was also subscribed to by François Fénelon, whom we have quoted before:

Without the actual inspiration of the spirit of grace, we can neither do, nor desire, nor believe anything good. Thus we are always inspired, but we continually stifle this inspiration. God does not cease speaking but the noise of the creature without, and of our passions within, deafens us and stops our hearing. We must silence every creature, we must silence ourselves, to hear in the deep hush of the whole soul, the ineffable voice of the spouse. We must bend the ear, because it is a gentle and delicate voice, only heard by those who no longer hear anything else.[31]

The use of silence is supported by almost every religious sect. Most stress silence in worship and in personal meditation. Many enforce hours or even days of silence as part of the regular retreat experience. Silence is especially important to the Quakers (Society of Friends), ever since it was introduced as a discipline by the founder, George Fox, in 1656.

> There is a danger and temptation to you in drawing your Minds into your Business and clogging them with it, so that you hardly do anything to the service of God, but there will be crying My Business, My Business and your minds will go into the things and not over the things, and so therein you do not come into the Image of God, which is dominion.[32]

In our day, silence was encouraged by Thomas Merton, Roman Catholic author, social activist, and spiritual counselor. He wrote for the lay person as well as the monk, so what he had to say about the monastic discipline is applicable to secular life.

> The Christian solitary, in his life of prayer and silence, explores the existential depths and possibilities of his own life. . . . The Christian solitary is left alone with God to fight out the questions of who he really is, to get rid of the impersonation, if any, that has followed him into the woods. . . . The silence of the woods forces you to make a decision which the tensions and artificialities of society may help you to evade forever.[33]

Later in the same chapter on Christian Solitude, Merton observed: "The man who can live happily without snuggling up at every moment to some person, institution or vice, is there as a promise of freedom for the rest of men."

Silence is not just being in a quiet place. Nor is it a mind that has been emptied of all anxieties. Silence means that outer as well as inner distractions to the Spirit have been overcome. Silence is a condition of the soul which has achieved peace, though it may still live in crowded conditions. Genuine silence is the presence of the Presence.

Notes

1. Margaret Cropper, *Evelyn Underhill* (New York: Harper & Row, 1958), p. 90.

2. *Ibid.*, p. 95.

3. William Law, *A Serious Call to a Devout and Holy Life,* ed. John W. Meister (Philadelphia: Westminster Press, 1975), p. 92.

4. Thomas R. Kelly, *A Testament of Devotion* (New York: Harper & Bros., 1941), pp. 59–61.

5. Thomas Merton, *Spiritual Direction and Meditation* (Collegeville, Minn.: Liturgical Press, 1959), p. 21.

6. Francis de Sales, *Introduction to a Devout Life* (Cleveland: World, 1952), Pt. I, No. 4, p. 34.

7. Mary Cooper Robb, *The Life of Christian Devotion: Devotional Selections from the Works of William Law* (New York: Abingdon, 1961), p. 79.

8. Jeremy Taylor, *The Rule and Exercises of Holy Living* (Cleveland: World, 1956), p. 4.

9. Friedrich von Hügel, *Selected Letters* (London: Dent, 1927), p. 229.

10. *Ibid.,* p. 201.

11. Brother Lawrence, *The Practice of the Presence of God* (New York: Fleming H. Revell, 1895), 1st Letter, p. 31.

12. *Ibid.,* 6th Letter.

13. Dietrich Bonhoeffer, *Letters and Papers from Prison,* tr. Reginald Fuller et al. (New York: Macmillan, paperback, enlarged edition, 1972), pp. 362, 381.

14. John Baillie, *Christian Devotion* (New York: Scribner's, 1962), p. 42.

15. Thomas S. Kepler, ed., *Theologica Germanica* (Cleveland: World, 1952), p. 68.

16. Martin Luther, *Table Talk,* ed. Thomas S. Kepler (New York: World, 1952).

17. Thomas R. Kelly, *A Testament of Devotion, op. cit.,* p. 60.

18. William Law, *Christian Perfection,* ed. Erwin Paul Rudolph (Carol Stream, Ill.: Creation House, 1975), p. 125.

19. Teresa of Avila, *The Way of Perfection,* tr. and ed. E. Allison Peers (Garden City, N.Y.: Doubleday, 1972).

20. Brother Lawrence, *The Practice of the Presence of God, op. cit.,* 8th Letter, p. 50.

21. François Fénelon, *On Prayer and Meditation* (New York: Harper & Bros., 1947).

22. Teresa of Avila, *The Way of Perfection, op. cit.*

23. Friedrich von Hügel, *The Life of Prayer* (New York: Dutton, 1929).

24. ———, *Selected Letters, op. cit.,* p. 304.

25. ———, *The Life of Prayer, op. cit.*

26. Attributed to St. Francis of Assisi.

27. Thomas Merton, *Spiritual Direction and Meditation, op. cit.,* p. 43.

28. *Ibid.,* p. 53.

29. Douglas Steere, *Prayer and Worship* (New York: Association, 1938), p. 67.

30. Thomas à Kempis, *Imitation of Christ* (Cleveland: World, 1956), Bk. 1, Ch. 20.

31. François Fénelon, *Christian Perfection,* tr. Mildred. W. Stillman (New York: Harper & Bros., 1947), p. 155.

32. George Fox, *Journal,* ed. Thomas S. Kepler (Nashville: Upper Room, 1951).

33. Thomas Merton, *Contemplation in a World of Action* (Garden City, N.Y.: Doubleday, 1971), p. 244.

3

THE PRESENCE
AS AN INFLUENCE
TOWARD PERSONAL
AND SOCIAL CHANGE

Up to this point, I have sought to explore the Presence as an important part of life. I have documented how It has been experienced by men and women through the centuries up to the present time. I have offered a number of ways in which It may be cultivated.

It is now extremely important to discuss how we may practice this rich spiritual experience.

Of course, different people practice the Presence in different ways. There is no one recommended method. And probably no "best" way. But there are at least two courses of action that should be considered. Each has stood the test of time and is still popular today. Each course contrasts sharply with the other.

One is to pursue your own *personal sanctification*. This means being concerned with your own personal piety. It means deepening your worship and prayer life. It means strengthening your own faith. It means changing yourself so that then you can influence the world around you.

The other is to *lose yourself in serving the needs of your neighbor*. It means stressing Works rather than Faith. It means changing social conditions so that they will, in turn, have a more positive influence upon individuals. It means being action-minded about religion. It means confronting those social, moral, and economic evils that are blighting lives.

Both of these ways of practicing the Presence have their champions. Both have a multitude of followers. Let us deal with each one in turn.

The Pursuit of Personal Piety

There is a dramatic story in the New Testament about a visit of Jesus in the home of two sisters, Martha and Mary.

Apparently Jesus was met at the door by Martha, who continued to welcome Him with "much serving." On the other hand, Mary "sat at His feet" and spent her time listening to what He had to say.

Later Jesus remarked about the difference between the two women. "Martha," he observed, "you are anxious and troubled about many things, but one thing is needful." Then, turning to Mary he added, "Mary has chosen the good portion which shall not be taken away from her" (see Luke 10:38–42).

Many believers in the Christian life feel directed by Jesus to accept the role of Mary. They understand that He expects those who follow Him to have a personal sense of devotion and to listen attentively to His teachings. They reiterate: "Mary has chosen the good portion"—silence and contemplation, which Christ preferred, in contrast to "much serving." They therefore conclude that intimate discipleship with the Lord is the authentic style of the Christian way of life.

This attitude epitomizes one of the most popular types of Christian faith. For centuries, monks and nuns have left the world and all its posessions to study the life and teachings of Jesus. At mountain or desert retreats, they have spent long hours and pursued intense disciplines in order to "fill their souls with peace." They have engaged in vigils of silence to gain an inner "marvelous sweetness." They have found their minds "simplified and tranquilized by God." Indeed, such spiritual devotion sometimes produced exciting visions of the body and face of Jesus. Thus, through what has been called "mysticism," people have discovered pathways to closer union with God.

They have, of course, always been concerned with the poor and the sick as well; but these good works were often considered secondary compared to meditation and retreat.

In today's world, mysticism plays a less popular role. But personal piety continues to hold a prime place in the religious life. Many voices, as well as sound experiences, argue for its importance. I have heard spiritual leaders say:

"I must first accept the Lord in my own heart, before I can lead others to him."

"Christ went about saving souls, not changing society."

"Be true to yourself and you shall not be false to anyone."

"Renew the world spiritually, beginning with me."

"Change the individual first and he or she will change others."

"God is concerned with the soul. He seeks to save us all, one by one."

The Pursuit of Good Works

A very different model of Christian discipleship is presented in the Letter of James.

> What does it profit, my brethren, if a man says he has faith but has not works? Can this faith save him? If a brother or sister is ill-clad and in lack of daily food, and one of you says to them, "Go in peace, be warmed and filled," without giving them the things needed for the body, what does it profit? So faith by itself, if it has no works, is dead.
>
> James 2:14–17

From this scripture, and others like it, we are led to believe that not piety but works is the important part of the Christian Way. In fact, some people are convinced that

Jesus supports activity in contrast to piety and that He said so in His conversation about the Last Judgment when He was at the Mount of Olives.

> Then the King shall say to those at his right hand . . . "I was hungry and you gave me food, I was thirsty and you gave me drink, I was a stranger and you welcomed me. . . ."
> Then the righteous will answer him, "Lord, when did we see thee hungry and feed thee or thirsty and give thee drink?"
> Then the King will answer them, . . . "as you did it unto one of the least of these my brethren, you did it to me."
> Matthew 25:34–40

Thus many Christians can find scriptural sources which call them to a life of service and social concern for those in need. They conclude that personal piety without good works really amounts to nothing. Faith, they claim, must be validated by Works. When Faith does express itself in action, in Christ's name, then it fulfills the teaching of Scripture.

The Importance of Faith and Works Together

It is my conviction that Faith and Works should be equal parts of the practice of the Presence. Unfortunately, this is not always the case.

In the one extreme, the pietist (the person who puts personal salvation before anything else) appears too ready to withdraw from responsibility for changing evil social conditions. The other extreme, the activist (the person who believes that social change will bring about individual change), appears to downgrade the role of worship, prayer, and spiritual power.

In reality, the pietist and the activist need each other, although each finds it difficult to accept the truths of the other's convictions. As we have pointed out, Faith without Works is deadening to the human spirit. Works without the influence of Faith are often shortlived and loveless.

When each side isolates itself and excludes the other, spiritual development is constricted. All too often the pietists' appeal for wider acceptance by the public is rejected because they appear narrowminded and uninterested in attacking the evils afflicting so many persons. In like manner, the activists could be more effective and gain greater churchwide support for their work if they would acknowledge and seek interior strengths from prayer and worship.

Faith needs the practicality of Works to keep it honest, and Works need the sustaining power produced by Faith. Faith needs the everyday experience of Works to keep it relevant; Works need the spiritual foundation of Faith in order to endure. The person who is obedient to both of these traditions stands the better chance of fully practicing the Presence.

Two observations need to be made at this point. First, when our Lord spoke in the synagogue, He proclaimed His mission as being both preaching the faith and practicing it: "The Spirit of the Lord is upon me because he has anointed me to preach good news to the poor . . . and to set at liberty those who are oppressed."

Second, when Jesus chose two people to exemplify the intent of His message, He chose sisters! Activity and devotion are related to each other.

What Some Religious Authorities Have Said About the Relationship of Faith and Works

Meister Eckhart (1260–1328). Eckhart was one of the significant influences on Western mystical thought in the thirteenth century. He was, at the same time, a champion of social change who laid the groundwork for better hospital and school systems in the Low Countries of Europe.

> The active life is contemplation. One must root himself in this soil of contemplation to make himself fruitful in works. The object of contemplation is then achieved. God's purpose in contemplation is to lead one to the accomplishment of fruitful works whereby many are saved in love.[1]

Francis de Sales (1567–1622). De Sales is the author of the spiritual masterpiece *Introduction to a Devout Life*. He is certainly one of the experts on the life of the Presence.

> If you undertake the devout life, you must not only cease from sin, but also cleanse your heart from all affection to sin; for these wretched affections will so perpetually depress your spirits that they will render you incapable of practising good works with alacrity and diligence: in which nevertheless, consist the very essence of devotion.[2]

Evelyn Underhill (1875–1941). No recent woman has written with more authority on the topic of the spiritual life and the Presence than Evelyn Underhill:

> Without the inner life of prayer and meditation, lived for its own sake and for no utilitarian motive, neither our judgements upon the social order nor our active social service will be perfectly performed; because they will not be the channel

of Creative Spirit expressing itself through us in the world of today.[3]

Thomas Merton (1915–1968). One of the outstanding exponents of the contemplative life in our time, Merton is probably read by more people than any other contemporary Roman Catholic author.

He who attempts to act and do things for others . . . without deepening his own self understanding, freedom, integrity and capacity to love, will not have anything to give others. He will communicate to them nothing but the contagion of his own obsessions. . . . We are living through the greatest crisis in the history of man; and this crisis is centered precisely in the country that has made a fetish out of action, and has lost the sense of contemplation. Far from being irrelevant, prayer, meditation and contemplation are of the utmost importance in America today.[4]

Notes

1. Thomas Katsares, *Western Mystical Tradition* (New Haven: Yale University Press, 1969).
2. Francis de Sales, *Introduction to a Devout Life* (Cleveland: World, 1952), p. 45.
3. Thomas S. Kepler, ed., *The Evelyn Underhill Reader* (Nashville: Abingdon, 1962), p. 69.
4. Thomas Merton, *Contemplation in a World of Action* (Garden City, N.Y.: Doubleday, 1971), p. 164.

4

SOME CAUTIONS
ABOUT
CULTIVATION

Introduction

In Chapter 2, I mentioned a number of different methods by which the Presence may be cultivated. Not all of them may speak to your spiritual needs, but some of them must be followed if you are to make progress on your pilgrimage of faith.

Now, before you begin to set up the plan you want to follow, it will be important to note some of the dangers ahead. In this chapter, I list seven "cautions" which you would do well to consider. They come from the wisdom of first-century Christians, from the mystics of the fourteenth and fifteenth centuries, and from the experiences of recent men and women.

The "cautions" I refer you to are not just matters of application or program but are the more serious dangers of attitude, upon the mastery of which so much real spiritual progress depends.

Some Cautions About the Cultivation Process

1. Attention to the interior life should never be seen as a way of avoiding responsibility for the world. It is true that pursuit of the Spirit often calls us "out of the world"—but only to the extent that we can discover greater strengths and truths in order to return to the reality of life and improve it.

A close look at the lives of many significant spiritual-life people reveals the fact that often social awareness comes from spiritual insight. The social concern for the poor of the Franciscans is founded on the spiritual life of St. Francis.

The social commitment of the Society of Friends (Quakers) comes out of the religious experience of George Fox. The concern of the Methodist Church for social conditions stems from the evangelical religious fervor of John Wesley.

Evelyn Underhill, to whom I have referred, who has proven herself as a teacher about the spiritual life by her constant writings on the topic, suggests:

> It is far easier, though not very easy, to develop and preserve a spiritual outlook on life, than it is to make our everyday actions harmonize with that spiritual outlook. That means, trying to see things, people, choices from the angle of eternity; and dealing with them as part of the material in which the Spirit works. This will be decisive for the way we behave as to our personal, social and national obligations. It will decide the papers we read, the movements we support. . . .
>
> Therefore the prevalent notion that spirituality and politics have nothing to do with each other is the exact opposite of truth. Once it is accepted in a realistic sense, the Spiritual Life has everything to do with politics. It means that certain convictions about God and the world become the moral and spiritual imperatives of our life; and this must be decisive for the way we choose to behave about that bit of the world over which we have been given limited control.[1]

2. There is no method or discipline or system of any kind that can ever command the Spirit to be present. At first glance, it seems that several famous "religious" have urged set procedures as though they were prerequisites to Faith. Ignatius Loyola established rigorous orders by his *Spiritual Exercises* and suggested that faithful pursuit of them would reward the seeker, but he never suggested that the orders would guarantee the Presence. John Baillie, the popular

English mystic, called for adherence to established religious disciplines but he did not go so far as to claim that the method would guarantee the Presence.

The Presence of God can never be forced, of course, and nothing in this manual should be construed to assume that it can be. This truth is well described by Blaise Pascal, a Roman Catholic religious mystic of the seventeenth century, who, during an illness, wrote the following prayer to God:

> neither discourses nor books,
> neither your Sacred Scripture, nor your Gospel,
> neither your holiest mysteries,
> neither alms nor fasts,
> neither mortification nor miracles,
> neither the use of the Sacraments
>   nor the sacrifice of your Body
> can do anything at all to bring about my conversion,
> unless you accompany all those things
> with the wholly extraordinary help of your grace.[2]

The best that any method can do is to help us become more open and sensitive so that we can receive more of the meaning of the Spirit. The most elaborate programs of spiritual development, no matter how faithfully followed, will always prove inadequate.

3. There is danger in believing that a faithful practice of any spiritual discipline will make us better than other people. Certainly it is commendable to seek the spiritual life in order to become a better person, but some very interesting perspectives soon appear.

The more a person becomes experienced in any field of endeavor, the more he or she becomes aware of how much there really is to know. Thus the wisest person is the one who knows that he or she is not wise. And it is the same with the saint. Because the saint has been pursuing the meanings of life, the saint knows how much there is to the spiritual life that he or she does not know. It is the saint who is aware, far better than the novice, how far short of the perfection of God life can actually be. Thus it was natural for the apostle Paul to exclaim with the insight of a saint that he was "the chief among sinners."

Of course, the real competition in life is not so much with my neighbor as it is with myself. I will be judged on what I have done with my life, not on what I have done with my neighbor's life. Søren Kierkegaard made a great point of the individual accountability of each person in his *Purity of Heart*. He reminds us that when we stand before God, the question will not be "what did you do with your neighbor's life?" for we have little control over that, but "what did you do with your life?" for which we are totally accountable.

Thus the matter is not whether cultivation of the Presence makes us better than our neighbor. The concern is whether or not it has made you and me better than ourselves. Has it helped to "kill the old man" inside and replace him or her with a "new creature"? The real question is not whether we win over our neighbor but whether we win over ourselves.

From another point of view, the question about becoming superior to our neighbor is interesting. If our motive is to be superior or better, then we have introduced the sin of Pride, which would set back whatever spiritual advance more pursuit of the Presence might have brought us.

4. We can never assume that the attainment of the spiritual life is a matter of education and intelligence. Although education and intelligence can be helpful, the Spirit finally is a matter of the soul and not of the mind. In fact, education and intelligence can be obstacles if they distract from the periods of meditation and if they are used as devices to capture the Spirit (which, of course, they cannot do). Indeed, the anonymous author of *The Cloud of Unknowing* stressed that even memory and tradition can be impediments. Receiving the Presence, the author felt, was a condition of becoming free from all previous mental attachments of any kind.

> For the love of God, be careful in this work, and do not, by any means, work in it with your mind or with your imagination: for, I tell you, it cannot be achieved with them. Therefore, leave them alone and do not work with them.[3]

Thomas Merton makes the same point about the difference between mind and soul:

> From the very start, it must be made clear that reflection does not refer to a purely intellectual activity, and still less does it refer to mere reasoning. Reflection involves not only the mind but our whole being. One who meditates does not merely think, he also loves.
>
> We need only remark that a person would be wasting his time if he thought reasoning alone could satisfy the need of his soul for spiritual meditation. Meditation is not merely a matter of "thinking things through," even if that leads to a good ethical resolution. Meditation is more than mere practical thinking.
>
> Meditation is for those who are not satisfied with a merely objective and conceptual knowledge about life,

about God, about ultimate realities. They want to enter into an intimate contact with truth itself, with God.[4]

Merton stresses this point when he adds, "meditation is generated not by reasoning but by faith."

5. The Roman Catholic has advantages over the Protestant in the cultivation of the Presence. If we accept 1517, the date on which Martin Luther posted the ninety-five theses on the door of the church at Wittenberg, as the beginning of the Protestant part of the Christian Church, then it will become readily apparent that the Roman Catholics have been cultivating the Presence far longer than their Protestant brethren. St. Augustine wrote his *Confessions* in 399. St. Francis had already begun his spiritual Order in 1212. St. Ignatius had written his *Spiritual Exercises* in 1522. Indeed, Roman Catholics are far ahead of the new Protestants in their search and discovery of the Presence.

In her book *The Protestant Mystics,* Anne Fremantle captures the differences between the Roman Catholic and the Protestant approach to the Presence:

Catholic mystics travel a well-worn, well-known, well-marked and easily identifiable road .... the slow painful clearly marked journey is the same; the dark night of the senses, the purifications, the progress from petitionary prayer to meditation, from meditation to contemplation, from contemplation to infused prayer ... and thence, for the proficient ... to unitive prayer, to the mystic marriage, and, finally, to the state of union.

But for the mystic who happens to be Protestant, although he is not more isolated than the Catholic, the flight is always (as Plotinus calls it) from the *a*lone to the *A*lone. ... The fellow-climbers are not roped.

For the Catholic there are recognitions everywhere. But for [Protestants like] Jacob Boehme, John Wesley or George Fox, there was no benefit of clergy, no scaffolding to hold on to, few guidebooks and little history to help.[5]

6. Using drugs as a method for cultivating the Presence is a danger to be avoided. Using drugs to expand the mind and soul beyond their "earthly limitations" has been traditionally pursued by a large number of people. For example, psychedelic drugs have been used in India for centuries. In the American Southwest, the Indians chew the buttonlike tops of the mescal cactus, or peyote, in their religious ceremonies to induce the feeling of exhilaration and otherworldliness.

William James, the American psychologist, in his masterpiece of religious types, *Varieties of Religious Experience,* indicates that drugs have the effect of producing mystical experiences, though he does not endorse them.

More recently and with the greater availability of drugs in America, their use as a producer of mystical ecstasy has increased. Among the most popular are alcohol, cocaine, PCP, LSD and THC—the active ingredient in marijuana.

What can be said for or against the use of drugs to achieve a mystical experience?

Those who support their use remind us that drugs have been resorted to for centuries with satisfying results. Drugs bring about expanded mind-consciousness upon command. They produce results which are extraordinary and attainable in no other way.

On the other hand, it should be noted that drugs have a negative physical effect. "Trips" are quite temporary and they are often accompanied by debilitating aftereffects. Such is not the case with a religious ecstasy. It is positive and enriching to both health and spirit. Its enjoyment is more permanent. Those who experience the mystical Presence have new physical powers; they "mount up as eagles," they walk and do not faint.

The use of drugs as creators of mystical ecstasy is questionable for other reasons. Any experience which must have an artificial basis seems tainted by its own origin. To become addicted to artificial stimuli, even to accomplish the best of objectives, raises serious questions. Furthermore, when personal euphoria is sought through drugs, the motive is usually self-gratification. The true classical spiritual rapture centers on the Presence of God rather than on a feeling of personal pleasure. The difference is critical.

For the cultivation of the Presence, drugs are not to be used in any form.

7. As spiritual values become clearer, the choice between good and evil patterns of living becomes more time-consuming and more painful. Often an intense struggle will take place before a new level of moral, ethical, or spiritual achievement is attained. An excellent example of such an inner battle has been described in the New Testament by the apostle Paul. He was a relatively good man struggling with the decision to lift his life to a different level. Even Paul found the change demanded all his strength and courage. It even seemed as though that was not enough.

> I do not understand my own actions. For I do not do what I want, but I do the very thing I hate. Now if I do what I do not want, I agree that the law is good . . . so then it is no longer I that do it, but sin which dwells within me. For I

know that nothing good dwells within me, that is, in my flesh. I can will what is right, but I cannot do it. For I do not do the good I want, but the evil I do not want is what I do. Now if I do what I do not want, it is no longer I that do it, but sin which dwells within me.

So I find it to be a law that when I want to do right, evil lies close at hand. For I delight in the law of God, in my inmost self, but I see in my members another law at war with the law of my mind and making me captive to the law of sin which dwells in my members. Wretched man that I am. Who will deliver me from this body of death?

Romans 7:15–24

The seeker for a different life should remember that bishops were (and are) not immune from these violent inner battles. St. Augustine describes his conflict in *Confessions,* which is a confession to God for being forgiven for his old life and being accepted in a new one.

The new will which I now began to have, by which I will to worship you freely and to enjoy You, O God, the only certain joy, was not yet strong enough to overcome that earlier will rooted deep through the years. My two wills, one old, one new, one carnal, one spiritual, were in conflict and in their conflict wasted my soul.

Thus with myself as object of the experiment, I came to understand what I had read, how the flesh lusts against the spirit and the spirit against the flesh. I indeed was in both camps.[6]

St. Teresa, one of the outstanding mystics of the early Church, a woman who became a spiritual guide to thousands, reports on her personal battles:

On the one side, God was calling me; on the other, I was following the world. All of the things of God gave me great pleasure and I was prisoner to things of the world. It seemed as if I wished to reconcile two contradictions as much at variance with each other as are the life of the Spirit and the joys, pleasures and amusement of sense.

I passed nearly twenty years on this stormy sea, falling and rising, but rising to no good purpose seeing that I went and fell again.[7]

Jacob Boehme, spiritual leader in Germany in the sixteenth century and founder of a movement that maintained hospitals, schools, and hostels for almost a century, reveals the difficulty he faced in choosing new values:

Finding within myself a great contrarium, namely the desires that belong to flesh and blood, I began to fight a hard battle against my corrupted nature; and with the aid of God, I made up my mind to overcome the inherited evil will, to brake it and to enter fully into the love of God.

This, however, was not possible for me to accomplish, but I stood firmly in my earnest resolution, and fought a hard battle with myself.

Now while I was wrestling and battling, being aided by God, a wonderful light arose in my soul. It was a light entirely foreign to my unruly nature, but in it I recognized the true nature of God and man, and the relation existing between them, a thing which heretofore I had never understood.[8]

Another typical, but outstanding example of the struggle of soul is most graphically found in John Bunyan's *Grace Abounding to the Chief of Sinners:*

• As a youth, he could ''sin with the greatest delight and ease.''

• Later his wife introduced him to books which included *The Plain Man's Pathway to Heaven.*

- He considered the religious life, but was afraid that "heaven was gone already" and his personal interest too late for God's attention.

- He began to attend worship services but found "it a full year before I could leave dancing."

- Again he wondered if "the day of grace was past and gone."

- He worried "lest Christ shoud have no liking for me."

- He kept falling back into struggles between good and evil.

- He often felt that "all comfort was taken from me, darkness seized upon me, after which whole floods of blasphemies, both against God, Christ and the scriptures, flooded over me."

- He found peace once again in the words from Romans: "if God be with us, who can be against us."

- He again vacillated between peace and depression and had a great desire to "sell Christ."

- He would so want to escape the claim of Christ on his life that he would reject Him by crying, "Sell Him, sell Him, sell Him."

- He often identified himself with Peter, who renounced Christ.

- Through various Scriptures and self-discipline, he finally found peace and inner acceptance.[9]

It should be reassuring, as you search for values that are more meaningful and rewarding than those you now follow, to know that inner struggle has been the common experience of most religious leaders.

Indeed, it has been only *because they have struggled* that

they have achieved their significant insights. The inner battle is necessary. It is the process of change. The dross of a previous life must be "burned away" in the heat of conflict before a new person can come forth.

The preceding illustrations suggest that:

1. Even the "best" of religious leaders have passed through difficult inner struggles in their growth toward peace and commitment. We should not be discouraged if we, too, experience painful trials and temptations.

2. These periods of inner conflict need not be seen as "weakness" but, rather, can be seen as "progress." Development of a more spiritual life and greater concern for others often does not happen unless an inner battle over values has taken place.

3. The time of inner turmoil can be the burning of self-will. By such a process, a person redirects his or her attention from concern about self to concern about the needs of others. We must change from "my will be done" to "Thy Will be done" in order to grow in the Plan of God.

4. Thus, "heaven" is often entered through the cleansing fires of a condition described as "hell." In this sense, hell can be the passage to heaven.

5. The inner battle does not have to be fought all alone. How many times we hear people say, "A strange power came into my life and I quit smoking," or "A 'Guardian Angel' has helped me overcome being judgmental," or "If it were not for the help I get from prayer, I would be the most selfish person alive." Time and again, we hear testimonies of some extraordinary power coming into our lives. It may be called the Presence.

Notes

1. Evelyn Underhill, *The Spiritual Life* (New York: Harper & Bros., 1936), p. 80.

2. E. Glenn Hinson, *Seekers After Mature Faith* (Texas: Word, 1968). A quotation from Blaise Pascal, *Pensées,* tr. M. Turnell (London: Burns and Oates, 1961), pp. 189–90.

3. *The Cloud of Unknowing,* tr. Ira Progoff (New York: Julian Press, 1969), p. 69.

4. Thomas Merton, *Spiritual Direction and Meditation* (Collegeville, Minn.: Liturgical Press, 1960), p. 43.

5. Anne Fremantle, *The Protestant Mystics* (Boston: Little, Brown, 1964).

6. St. Augustine, *Confessions,* tr. F. J. Sheed (New York: Sheed & Ward, 1942), p. 135.

7. Teresa of Avila, *Autobiography,* tr. and ed. E. Allison Peers (New York: Doubleday, 1973).

8. Rufus Jones, *Spiritual Reformers of the Sixteenth Century* (Boston: Beacon, 1959), p. 201.

9. Summarized from John Bunyan, *Grace Abounding to the Chief of Sinners* (Chicago: Allenson, 1955).

5

EXCERPTS FROM
TWENTY-ONE
SIGNIFICANT BOOKS
OF THE PRESENCE

In the preceding chapters, I have considered the various methods by which the Presence may be cultivated. I have stressed the importance of combining Faith and Works by pointing out that some of the most authentic religious leaders kept mystical inspiration and social commitment in balance. I have also listed a number of Cautions, e.g., attitudes which could prove dangerous.

Let us turn now to some outstanding examples of devotional material. I have included in this chapter excerpts from books that can be considered classics.

I have chosen each selection because it expresses the literary quality of the author. Each example is an entity in and of itself, presenting an entire idea or event. Each excerpt has been chosen because it reveals the spirit and style of the author.

This chapter has two objectives. The first is to introduce you to original source material with the hope that you will find those authors which appeal to your interests and needs. The second is to provide you with a number of readings which you can use for your own devotions. But as you do so, it would be well to observe one condition. Do not read any classic only once and feel you understand it or have found all of its power. Each excerpt, like all devotional material, contains far more meaning than at first appears. Read repeatedly so that the author can speak to your soul.

If you decide, after using these brief samples, that you want to do more meditation with the support of other excellent daily devotions, I suggest *A Diary of Readings* by John Baillie (365 different and superb meditations by many authors). Try also *A Devotional Treasury from the Early Church* (memorable samples of early Christian faith) edited by Georgia Harkness. You will also enjoy *The Choice Is Always Ours,* "an anthology of the religious way," edited by Dorothy Berkley Phillips. Don't overlook *The Protestant Mystics* by Anne Fremantle, and *Search for Silence* by Elizabeth O'Connor.

Two other authors should be mentioned: Douglas Steere, who has written a great deal about spiritual-life retreats, the relationship of work and contemplation, and who has kept the public aware of many of the classic books of devotion; and Thomas S. Kepler, likewise a champion of the spiritual life and editor of an extraordinarily helpful series of pocket-sized pamphlets called *Living Selections from the Great Devotional Classics*—about twenty-five in all, from St. Augustine to Dietrich Bonhoeffer.

Selections of Writings on the Presence

A DIARY OF PRIVATE PRAYER
FIRST DAY . . . MORNING

John Baillie

Eternal Father of my soul, let my first thought today be of Thee, let my first impulse be to worship Thee, let my first speech be Thy name, let my first action be to kneel before Thee in prayer.

> For Thy perfect wisdom and perfect goodness:
> For the love wherewith Thou lovest mankind:
> For the love wherewith Thou lovest me:
> For the great and mysterious opportunity of my life:
> For the indwelling of Thy Spirit in my heart:
> For the sevenfold gifts of Thy spirit:
> > I worship and praise Thee, O Lord.

Yet let me not, when this morning prayer is said, think my worship ended and spend the day in forgetfulness of Thee. Rather from these moments of quietness let light go forth, and joy, and power, that will remain with me through all the hours of the day;

> Keeping me chaste in thought:
> Keeping me temperate and truthful in speech:
> Keeping me faithful and diligent in my work:
> Keeping me humble in my estimation of myself:
> Keeping me honourable and generous in my dealings with others:
> Keeping me loyal to every hallowed memory of the past:
> Keeping me mindful of my eternal destiny as a child of Thine.

O God, who hast been the Refuge of my fathers through many generations, be my Refuge today in every time and circumstance of need. Be my Guide through all that is dark and doubtful. By my Guard against all that threatens my spirit's welfare. Be my Strength in time of testing. Gladden my heart with Thy peace; through Jesus Christ my Lord. Amen.

A DEVOTIONAL TREASURY FROM THE EARLY CHURCH
THE LETTER TO DIOGNETUS
Edited by Georgia Harkness

For Christians cannot be distinguished from the rest of the human race by country or language or customs. They do not live in cities of their own; they do not use a particular form of speech, they do not follow an eccentric manner of life. This doctrine of theirs has not been discovered by the ingenuity or deep thought of inquisitive men, nor do they put forward a merely human teaching, as some people do. Yet, although they live in Greek and barbarian cities alike, as each man's lot has been cast, and follow the customs of the country in clothing and food and other matters of daily living, at the same time they give proof of the remarkable and admittedly extraordinary constitution of their own commonwealth. They live in their own countries, but only as aliens. They have a share in everything as citizens, and endure everything as foreigners. Every foreign land is their fatherland, and yet for them every fatherland is a foreign land. They marry, like everyone else, and they beget children, but they do not cast out their offspring. They share their board with each other, but not their marriage bed. It is true that they are ''in the flesh,'' but they do not live ''according to the flesh.'' They busy themselves on earth, but their citizenship is in heaven. They obey the established laws, but in their own lives they go far beyond what the laws require. They love all men, and by all men are persecuted. They are unknown, and still they are condemned; they are put to death, and yet they are brought to life. They are poor and yet they make many rich; they are completely destitute, and yet they enjoy complete abundance. They are dishonored, and in their very dishonor are glorified; they are defamed, and are vindicated. They are reviled, and yet they bless; when they are affronted, they still pay due respect. When they do good they are punished as evildoers; undergoing punishment, they rejoice because they are brought to life. They are treated by the Jews as foreigners and enemies, and are hunted down by the Greeks, and all the time those who hate them find it impossible to justify their enmity.

To put it simply: What the soul is in the body, that Christians are in the world. The soul is dispersed through all the members of the body, and Christians are scattered through all the cities of the world. The soul dwells in the body but does not belong to the body, and Christians dwell in the world but do not belong to the world. The soul which is invisible, is kept under guard in the visible body; in the same way, Christians are recognized when they are in the world, but their religion remains unseen. . . .

It is to no less a post than this that God has ordered them, and they must not try to evade it.

THE LIFE OF THE SPIRIT
AND THE LIFE OF TODAY
THE CHARACTERISTICS OF SPIRITUAL LIFE

Evelyn Underhill

The first point I wish to make is, that the experience which we call the life of the Spirit is such a genuine fact; which meets us at all times and places, and at all levels of life. It is an experience which is independent of, and often precedes, any explanation or rationalization. . . .

By three main ways we tend to realize our limited personal relationship with that transcendent Other. . . .

First, there is a profound sense of security; of being safely held in a cosmos of which, despite all contrary appearance, peace is the very heart. . . . God is the Ground of the soul, the Unmoved, our Very Rest; statements which meet us again and again in spiritual literature.

In the second characteristic form of the religious experience, the relationship is felt rather as the intimate and reciprocal communion of a person with a Person; a form of apprehension which is common to the great majority of devout natures. . . . For it is always in a personal and emotional relationship that man finds himself impelled to surrender to God; and this surrender is felt by him to evoke a response.

Last—and here is the aspect of religious experience which is specially to concern us—Spirit is felt as an overflowing power, a veritable accession of vitality; energizing the self, or the religious group, impelling it to the fullest and most zealous living-out of its existence, giving it fresh joy and vigour, and lifting it to fresh levels of life.

This sense of enhanced life is a mark of religions of the

Spirit. "He giveth power to the faint," says the Second Isaiah, "and to them that hath no might he increaseth strength. . . . they that wait upon the Lord shall renew their strength; they shall mount up with wings as eagles; they shall run and not be weary; and they shall walk and not faint."

"I live—yet not I," "I can do all things," says St. Paul, seeking to express his dependence on this Divine strength invading and controlling him.

"My life," says Augustine, "shall be a real life, being wholly full of Thee."

"Having found God," says a modern Indian saint, "the current of my life flowed on swiftly, I gained fresh strength." All other men and women of the Spirit speak in the same sense, when they try to describe the source of their activity and endurance.

CONFESSIONS

St. Augustine

It is with no doubtful knowledge, Lord, but with utter certainty that I love you. You have stricken my heart with your word and I love you. And heaven and earth and all that is in them tell me wherever I look that I should love you, and they cease not to tell it to all men, so that there is no excuse for them. For you will have mercy on whom you will have mercy and you will show mercy to whom you will show mercy, otherwise heaven and earth cry their praise of you to deaf ears.

But what is it that I love when I love you?

Not the beauty of any bodily thing, nor the order of the seasons, nor the brightness of light that rejoices the eye, nor the sweet melodies of all songs, nor the sweet fragrance of flowers and ointments and spices; nor manna nor honey, not the limbs that carnal love embraces. None of these things do I love in loving my God. Yet in a sense I do love light and melody and fragrance and food and embrace in the soul, when that light shines upon my soul which no place can contain, that voice sounds which no time can take from me, I breathe that fragrance which no wind scatters, I eat the food which is not lessened by eating, and I lie in the embrace which satiety never comes to sunder. This is it that I love, when I love my God.

And what is this God?

I asked the earth and it answered: "I am not He."

I asked the sea and the deeps and the creeping things, and they answered: "We are not your God, seek higher."

I asked the winds that blow, and the whole air with all that is in it, answered: "Anaximenes was wrong; I am not God."

I asked the heavens, the sun, the moon, the stars, and they answered: "Neither are we God whom you seek."

And I said to all things that throng about the gateways of the senses: "Tell me of my God since you are not He. Tell me something of Him."

And they cried out in a great voice: "He made us."

My question was my gazing upon them, and their answer was their beauty. And I turned to myself and said: "And you. Who are you?" And I answered: "A man."

Now clearly there is a body and a soul in me, one exterior, one interior. From which of these two should I have enquired of my God? I had already sought him by my body, from earth to heaven, as far as my eye could send its beams on the quest. But the interior part is the better, seeing that all my body's messengers delivered to it, as ruler and judge, the answers that heaven and earth, and all things in them made when they said "We are not God" and "He made us." The inner man knows these things through the ministry of the outer man; I the inner man knew them, I, the soul, through the sense of the body. I asked the whole frame of the universe about my God and it answered me: "I am not He, but He made me."

JOURNAL
GREAT OPENINGS, GREAT TROUBLES
George Fox

Now though I had great openings, yet great trouble and temptation came many times upon me, so that when it was day I wished for night, and when it was night I wished for day; and by reason of the openings I had in my troubles, I could say as David said, "Day unto day uttereth speech, and night unto night showeth knowledge." And when I had openings, they answered one another and answered the Scriptures, for I had great openings of the Scriptures; and when I was in troubles, one trouble also answered to another.

But my troubles continued, and I was often under great temptations; and I fasted much, and walked abroad in solitary places many days, and often took my bible and went and sat in hollow trees and lonesome places till night came on; and frequently in the night walked mournfully about by myself, for I was a man of sorrows in the times of the first workings of the Lord in me.

JOURNAL
ON PRACTICAL FORGIVENESS
George Fox

The next first day I went to Tickhill, whither the Friends of that side gathered together. When Friends were in the meeting, and fresh and full of the life and power of God, I was moved to go out of the meeting to the steeplehouse; and when I came there, I found the priest and most of the chiefs of the parish together in the chancel. So I went up to them and began to speak; but they immediately fell upon me; and the clerk up with his Bible, as I was speaking, and struck me on the face with it, so that it gushed out with blood, and I bled exceedingly in the steeplehouse. Then the people cried, "Let us have him out of the church"; and when they had got me out, they beat me sore with books, fists and sticks, and threw me down over a hedge and into a close, and there beat me and threw me over again; and afterwards they dragged me through a house into the street, stoning and beating me as they drew me along, so that I was besmeared all over with blood and dirt.

They got my hat from me, which I never got again. Yet when I got upon my legs again, I declared to them the word of life, and shewed them the fruits of their teacher, and how they dishonoured Christianity. After a while I got into the meeting again amongst Friends; and the priest and the people coming by the house, I went forth with Friends into the yard, and there I spoke with the priest and the people.

The priest scoffed at us and called us Quakers. But the Lord's power was so over them, and the word of life was declared in such authority and dread to them, that the priest began trembling himself; and one of the people said "look how the priest trembles and shakes, he is turned a Quaker also!"

When the meeting was over, Friends departed; and I went without my hat to Balby, about seven or eight miles. Friends were much abused that day by the priest and his people; insomuch as some moderate justices hearing of it, two or three of them came, and sat at the town to hear and examine the business. And he that had shed my blood was afraid of having his hand cut off for striking me in the steeplehouse, but I forgave him, and would not appear against him.

IMITATION OF CHRIST
Thomas à Kempis

Lament and grieve, that you are:

So watchful over your outward senses,
     so often entangled with many vain fancies:
So much inclined to outward things,
     so negligent in things inward and spiritual:
So prone to laughter and unbridled mirth,
     so indisposed to tears and compunction:
So prompt to ease and pleasures of the flesh,
     so dull to strictness of life and zeal:
So curious to hear news and to see beautiful sights,
     so slack to embrace what is humble and low:

So covetous of abundance, to niggardly in giving,
    so fast in keeping:
So inconsiderate in speech,
    so reluctant to keep silence:
So uncomposed in manners,
    so fretful in action:
So eager about food,
    so deaf to the word of God:
In such a hurry to rest,
    so slow to labor:
So wakeful in vain conversation,
    so drowsy at sacred services:
So hasty to arrive at the end thereof,
    so inclined to be wandering and inattentive:
So negligent in the prayers,
    so lukewarm in celebrating the holy communion,
    so dry and heartless in receiving it:
So quickly distracted,
    so seldom wholly gathered into yourself:
So suddenly moved to anger,
    so apt to take displeasure against another:
So ready to judge,
    so severe to reprove:
So joyful in prosperity,
    so weak in adversity:
So often making good resolutions,
    and yet bring them at last to so poor effect:

These and other, defects being confessed and bewailed with
    sorrow and great displeasure at your own infirmity,
    make yourself a firm resolution always to be amending
    your life, and endeavor always after a further progress
    in holiness.

PILGRIM'S PROGRESS

John Bunyan

Christian then and his companion asked the men to go along with them: so they told them that they would. But, said they, you must obtain it by our own faith. So I saw in my dream, that they went on together till they came in sight of the gate.

Now I further saw, that betwixt them and the gate was a river; but there was no bridge to go over: the river was very deep. At the sight, therefore, of this river the pilgrims were much stunned; but the men that went with them said, you must go through, or you cannot come at the gate.

The pilgrims then began to inquire, if there was no other way to the gate? To which they answered, Yes; but there hath not any, save two, to wit, Enoch and Elijah, been permitted to tread that path since the foundation of the world, nor shall until the last trumpet shall sound. The pilgrims then, especially Christian, began to despond in their mind, and looked this way and that; but no way could be found by them, by which they might escape the river. Then they asked the men if the waters were all of a depth? They said, No; yet they could not help them in that case; for said they, you shall find it deeper or shallower, as you believe in the King of the place.

They then addressed themselves to the water, and, entering, Christian began to sink, and, crying out to his good friend Hopeful, he said, I sink in deep waters; the billows go over my head; all his waves go over me. Selah.

Then said the other, Be of good cheer, my brother; I feel the bottom, and it is good. Then said Christian, Ah! my friend, the sorrows of death have compassed me about, I shall not see the land that flows with milk and honey. And with that a great darkness and horror fell upon Christian, so that he could not see before him. Also here he in a great measure lost his senses, so that he could neither remember nor orderly talk of any of those sweet refreshments that he had met with in the way of his pilgrimage. But all the words that he spoke still tended to discover that he had horror of mind, and heart-fears that he should die in that river, and never obtain entrance in at the gate. Here also, as they that stood by perceived, he was much in the troublesome thoughts of the sins that he had committed, both since and before he began to be a pilgrim. It was also observed, that he was troubled with apparitions of hobgoblins and evil spirits; for ever and anon he would intimate so much by words.

Hopeful therefore here had much ado to keep his brother's head above water; yea, sometimes he would be quite gone down, and then, ere a while, he would rise up again half dead. Hopeful did also endeavour to comfort him, saying, Brother, I see the gate, and men standing by to receive us; but Christian would answer, 'Tis you, 'tis you they wait for; for you have been hopeful ever since I knew you. And so have you, said he to Christian. Ah, brother, (said he), surely if I was right, he would now arise to help me; but for my sins he hath brought me into the snare, and hath left me. Then said Hopeful, My brother, you have quite forgot the text, where it is said of the wicked, "There are no bands in their death, but their strength is firm; they are not troubled as other men, neither are they plagued like other men." These troubles and distresses that you go through in these waters, are no sign that God hath forsaken you; but are sent to try you, whether you will call to mind that which heretofore you have received of his goodness, and live upon him in your distresses.

Then I saw in my dream, that Christian was in a muse a while. To whom also Hopeful added these words, Be of good cheer, Jesus Christ maketh thee whole. And with that Christian brake out with a loud voice, Oh, I see him again! and he tells me, "When thou passest through the waters, I will be with thee; and through the rivers, they shall not overflow thee." Then they both took courage, and the enemy was after that as still as a stone, until they were gone over. Christian therefore presently found ground to stand upon, and so it followed that the rest of the river was but shallow: thus they got over.

THE RULE AND EXERCISES OF HOLY LIVING
MEANS OF HOPE AND REMEDIES
AGAINST DESPAIR
Jeremy Taylor

St. Bernard reckons divers principles of hope, by enumerating the instances of the Divine mercy: and we may by them reduce this rule to practice, in the following manner:

1. God hath preserved me from many sins; His mercies are infinite: I hope He will preserve me from more, and for ever.

2. I have sinned and God smote me not; His mercies are still over the penitent; I hope He will deliver me from all evils I have deserved. He hath forgiven me many sins of malice, and therefore surely He will pity my infirmities.

3. God visited my heart and changed it: He loves the work of His own hands, and so my heart is now become: I hope He will love this too.

4. When I repented He received me graciously: and therefore I hope, if I do my endeavor, He will totally forgive me.

5. He helped my slow and beginning endeavors: and therefore I hope He will lead me to perfection.

6. When He had given me something first, then He gave me more: I hope, therefore, He will keep me from falling, and give me the grace of perseverance.

7. He hath chosen me to be a disciple of Christ's institution; He hath elected me to His kingdom of grace; and therefore I hope also to the kingdom of His glory.

8. He died for me when I was His enemy; and therefore I hope He will save me when He hath reconciled me to Him and is become my friend.

9. God hath given us His Son: how should He not with Him give us all things else?

All these St. Bernard reduces to these three heads, as the instruments of all our hopes: 1) the charity of God adopting us; 2) the truth of His promises; 3) the power of His performance.

ON CONSIDERATION
Bernard of Clairvaux

Let me offer you my advice. If you give all your life and your wisdom to action and nothing to consideration, do I praise you? In this I praise you not . . . . action itself does belong altogether to other people, like him who was made all things to all men, I praise your humanity, but only on condition that it be complete. But how can it be complete if you yourself are left out? You too, are a man. So then, in order that your humanity may be entire and complete, let your bosom, which receives all, find room for yourself also . . . . all drink at the public fountain of your heart; and will you stand apart and thirst? . . . By all means let your waters stream down into the streets; let men and flocks and herds drink thereof, nay let the servants of Abraham give drink even to the camels; but among the rest do you yourself drink the water of your own well. "Let not a stranger," saith Scripture, "drink thereat!" Are you a stranger? To whom are you not a stranger, if you are one to yourself? In short if a man is bad to himself, to whom is he good?

Let your consideration begin with yourself, lest, while you neglect yourself, you waste your energy on other things. What does it profit you if you gain the whole world and lose your single self? Though you be wise, you lack wisdom to yourself, if you do not belong to yourself.

THE SONG OF SONGS
Bernard of Clairvaux

You ask, then, how I knew that He was present, since His ways are past finding out? Because the Word is living and effective, and as soon as ever He has entered into me, He has aroused my sleeping soul, and stirred and softened and pricked my heart, that hitherto was sick and hard as stone. He has begun to pluck up and destroy, to build and to plant, to water the dry places and shed light upon the dark, to open what was shut, to warm the chill, to make the crooked straight and the rough places plain; so that my soul has blessed the Lord and all that is within me praised His holy Name. Thus has the Bridegroom entered into me; my senses told me nothing of His coming, I knew that He was present only by the movement of my heart; I perceived His power, because it put my sins to flight and exercised a strong control on all my impulses. I have been moved to wonder at His wisdom too, uncovering my secret faults and teaching me to see their sinfulness: and I have experienced His gentleness and kindness in such small measure of amendment as I have achieved: and, in the renewal and remaking of the spirit of my mind—that is, my inmost being, I have beheld to some degree the beauty of His glory and have been filled with awe as I gazed at His manifold greatness.

CONFESSIONS OF JACOB BOEHME
Jacob Boehme

But when this had given me many a hard blow and repulse, doubtless from the Spirit, which had a great longing yearning towards me, at last I fell into a very deep melancholy and heavy sadness, when I beheld and contemplated the great Deep of this world, also the sun and stars, the clouds, rain and snow, and considered in my spirit the whole creation of the world.

Wherein then I found, in all things, evil and good, love and anger; in the inanimate creatures, in wood, stones, earth and the elements, as also in men and beasts.

Moreover I considered the little spark of light, man, what he should be esteemed for with God, in comparison of this great work and fabric of heaven and earth.

And finding that in all things there was evil and good, as well in the elements as in the creatures, and that it went as well in this world with the wicked as with the virtuous, honest and godly; also that the barbarous people had the best countries in their possession, and that they had more prosperity in their ways than the virtuous, honest and godly had; I was thereupon very melancholy, perplexed and exceedingly troubled, no Scripture could comfort or satisfy me though I was very well acquainted with it and versed therein; at which time the Devil would by no means stand idle, but was often beating into me many heathenish thoughts which I will here be silent in.

Yet when in this affliction and trouble I elevated my spirit (which then I understood very little or nothing at all what it was), I earnestly raised it up into God, as with a great storm or onset, wrapping up my whole heart and mind, as also all my thoughts and whole will and resolution, incessantly to wrestle with the Love and Mercy of God, and not to give over unless he blessed me, that is, unless he enlightened me with his Holy Spirit, whereby I might understand his will and be rid of my sadness. And then the Spirit did break through.

But when in my resolved zeal I gave so hard an assault, storm, and onset upon God and upon all the gates of hell, as if I had more reserves of virtue and power ready, with a resolution to hazard my life upon it (which assuredly were not in my ability without the assistance of the Spirit of God) suddenly my spirit did break through the gates of hell, even into the innermost moving of the Deity, and there I was embraced in love as a bridegroom embraces his dearly beloved bride.

The greatness of the triumphing that was in my spirit I

cannot express either in speaking or writing; neither can it be compared to any thing but that wherein life is generated in the midst of death. It is like the resurrection from the dead.

In this light my spirit suddenly saw through all, and in and by all, the creatures; even in herbs and grass it knew God, who he is and how he is and what his will is. And suddenly in that light my will was set on by a mighty impulse to describe the Being of God.

But because I could not presently apprehend the deepest movings of God and comprehend them in my reason, there passed almost twelve years before the exact understanding thereof was given me.

THE PRACTICE OF THE PRESENCE OF GOD
Brother Lawrence

Such was my beginning, and yet I must tell you that for the first ten years I suffered much. The apprehension that I was not devoted to God as I wished to be, my past sins always present in my mind, and the great unmerited favors which God did for me, were the matter and source of my sufferings. During this time I fell often, and rose again presently. It seemed to me that all creatures, reason, and God Himself were against me, and faith alone for me. I was troubled sometimes with thoughts that to believe I had received such favors was an effect of my presumption, which pretended to be at once where others arrive with difficulty; at other times, that it was a wilful delusion, and that there was no salvation for me.

When I thought of nothing but to end my days in these

troubles (which did not at all diminish the trust I had in God, and which served only to increase my faith), I found myself changed all at once; and my soul, which till that time was in trouble, felt a profound inward peace, as if she were in her center and place of rest.

Ever since that time I walk before God simply, in faith, with humility and with love, and I apply myself diligently to do nothing and think nothing that may displease Him. I hope that when I have done what I can, He will do with me what He pleases.

.   .   .   .

I have quitted all forms of devotion and set prayers but those to which my state obliges me. And I make it my business only to persevere in His holy presence, wherein I keep myself by a simple attention, and a general fond regard to God, which I may call an actual presence of God; or, to speak better, an habitual, silent, and secret conversation of the soul with God, which often causes me joys and raptures inwardly, and sometimes also outwardly, so great that I am forced to use means to moderate them and prevent their appearance to others.

In short, I am assured beyond all doubt that my soul has been with God above these thirty years. I pass over many things that I may not be tedious to you, yet I think it proper to inform you after what manner I consider myself before God, whom I behold as my King.

I consider myself as the most wretched of men, full of sores and corruption, and who has committed all sorts of crimes against his King. Touched with a sensible regret, I confess to Him all my wickedness, I ask His forgiveness, I abandon myself in His hands that He may do what He pleases with me. The King, full of mercy and goodness, very far from chastising me, embraces me with love, makes me eat at His table, serves me with His own hands, gives me the key of His treasures; He converses and delights Himself with me incessantly, in a thousand and a thousand ways, and treats me in all respects as His favorite. It is thus I consider myself from time to time in His holy presence.

LITTLE FLOWERS OF ST. FRANCIS
ON PERFECT JOY
Translated by Raphael Brown

One winter day, St. Francis was coming to St. Mary of the angels from Perugia with Brother Leo and the bitter cold made them suffer keenly. St. Francis called to Brother Leo, who was walking a bit ahead of him, and he said: "Brother Leo, even if the Friars Minor in every country give a great example of holiness and integrity and good edification, nevertheless write down and note carefully that perfect joy is not in that."

And when he had walked on a bit, St. Francis called him again, saying: "Brother Leo, even if a Friar Minor gives sight to the blind, heals the paralyzed, drives out devils, gives hearing back to the deaf, makes the lame walk, and restores speech to the dumb, and, what is still more, brings back to life a man who has been dead four days, write that perfect joy is not in that." . . .

Now when he had been talking this way for a distance of two miles, Brother Leo in great amazement asked him: "Father, I beg you in God's name to tell me what perfect joy is."

And St. Francis replied: "When we come to St. Mary of the angels, soaked by the rain and frozen by the cold, all soiled with mud and suffering from hunger, and we ring at the gate of the Place, and the brother porter comes and says angrily: 'Who are you?' and we say: 'We are two of your brothers.' And he contradicts us, saying: 'You are not telling the truth. Rather you are two rascals who go around deceiving people and stealing what they give to the poor. Go away!' And he does not open for us, but makes us stand outside in the snow and rain, cold and hungry, until night falls—then if we endure all those insults and cruel rebuffs patiently, without being troubled and without complaining, and if we reflect humbly and charitably that that porter really knows us and that God makes him speak against us, oh, Brother Leo, write that perfect joy is there.

"And if we continue to knock, and the porter comes out in anger, and drives us away with curses and hard blows like bothersome scoundrels, saying: 'Get away from here, you dirty thieves—go to the hospital! Who do you think you are? You certainly won't eat or sleep here!' And if we bear it patiently and take the insults with joy and love in our hearts, oh, Brother Leo, write that that is perfect joy.

"And if later, suffering intensely from hunger and painful cold, with night falling, we still knock and call, and crying loudly beg them to open for us and let us come in for the love of God, and he grows still more angry and says: 'Those fellows are bold and shameless ruffians. I'll give them what they deserve!' And he comes out with a knotty club, and grasping us by the cowl throws us onto the ground, rolling us in the mud and snow, and beats us with that club so much that he covers our bodies with wounds, if we endure all those evils and blows and insults with joy and patience reflecting that we must accept and bear the sufferings of the Blessed Christ patiently for love of Him, oh, Brother Leo, write: 'that is perfect joy.'"

THE SCALE OF PERFECTION
HOW TO ASCERTAIN WHETHER YOU LOVE YOUR FELLOW-CHRISTIAN
Walter Hilton

If you are not moved to anger and open dislike of a person, and feel no secret hatred which makes you despise, humiliate, or belittle him, then you are in perfect charity with your fellow-Christian. And if, the more he shams or harms you in word or act, the more pity and compassion you feel towards him, as you would feel towards one who was out of his right mind, then you are in perfect charity. And if you feel that you cannot find it in your heart to hate him, knowing love to be good in itself, but pray for him, help him, and desire his amendment—not only in words as hypocrites can do, but with heartfelt love—then you are in perfect charity with your fellow-Christian. St. Stephen possessed this perfect charity when he prayed for those who stoned him to death. And Christ called for this charity in all who desire to follow him perfectly when he said: "Love your enemies and do good to those who hate you; pray for those who persecute and slander you!" (Matt: 5:44).

Therefore, if you desire to follow Christ, imitate him in this matter. Learn to love your enemies and all sinners, for they are all your fellow-Christians. Remember how Christ loved Judas, who was both his deadly enemy and a wicked man. How patient Christ was with him, how kindly, how courteous and humble to one he knew to be worthy of damnation. Despite this he chose him to be his apostle, and sent him to preach with the other apostles. He gave him power to work miracles, he showed him the same loving friendship in word and deed as the other apostles. He washed his feet, he fed him with his precious body, and taught him as he did the other apostles. He did not openly expose or rebuke him, nor did he despise or speak ill of him, although he might justly have done all of these things. And to crown his crimes, at Jesus' arrest Judas kissed him and called him his friend. Christ showed all this charity to one he knew to be a traitor; yet in everything that he did there was no pretense or insincerity, but pure love and true charity. For although Judas, because of his wickedness, was unworthy to receive any gift from God or any sign of love, it was nevertheless right and fitting that our Lord should show himself in his true nature. For he is love and goodness, and therefore shows love and goodness towards all his creatures as he did towards Judas. I do not say that he loved Judas for his sins, or that he loved him as one of his chosen, as he loved St. Peter. But he loved him inasmuch as he was his creature, and gave him proofs of his love, if only he could have responded to them and amended.

PURITY OF HEART IS TO WILL ONE THING
WHAT THEN MUST I DO? LIVE AS AN "INDIVIDUAL."

Søren Kierkegaard

Each man himself, as an individual, should render his account to God. No third person dares venture to intrude upon this accounting between God and the individual. Yet the talk, by putting its question, dares and ought to dare, to remind man, in a way never to be forgotten, that the most ruinous evasion of all is to be hidden in the crowd in an attempt to escape God's supervision of him as an individual, in an attempt to get away from hearing God's voice as an individual. Long ago, Adam attempted this same thing when his evil conscience led him to imagine that he could hide himself among the trees. It may be even easier and more convenient, and more cowardly to hide oneself among the crowd in the hope that God should not be able to recognize one from the other. But in eternity each shall render account as an individual. That is, eternity will demand of him that he shall have lived as an individual. Eternity will draw out before his consciousness, all that he has done as an individual, he who had forgotten himself in noisy self-conceit. In eternity, he shall be brought to account strictly as an individual, he who intended to be in the crowd where there should be no such strict reckoning. Each one shall render account to God as an individual. The King shall render account as an individual; and the most wretched beggar, as an individual. No one may pride himself at being more than an individual, and no one despondently think he is not an individual, perhaps because here in earth's busyness he had not as much as a name, but was named after a number.

THE FREEDOM OF A CHRISTIAN

Martin Luther

"Have this mind among yourselves, which you have in Christ Jesus, who, though he was in the form of God, did not count equality with God a thing to be grasped, but emptied himself, taking the form of a servant, being born in the likeness of men. And being found in human form he humbled himself and became obedient unto death" (Phil.

2:5–8). This salutary word of the Apostle has been obscured for us by those who have not at all understood his words, "form of God," "form of a servant," "human form," "likeness of men," and have applied them to the divine and the human nature. Paul means this: Although Christ was filled with the form of God and rich in all good things so that he needed no work and no suffering to make him righteous and saved (for he had all this eternally) yet he was not puffed up by them and did not exalt himself above us and assume power over us, although he could rightly have done so; but, on the contrary, he so lived, labored, worked, suffered, and died that he might be like other men and in fashion and in actions be nothing else than a man, just as if he had need of all these things and had nothing of the form of God. But he did all this for our sake, that he might serve us and that all things which he accomplished in this form of a servant might become ours.

So a Christian, like Christ his head, is filled and made rich by faith and should be content with this form of God which he has obtained by faith; only, as I have said, he should increase this faith until it is made perfect. For this faith is his life, his righteousness, and his salvation: it saves him and makes him acceptable, and bestows upon him all things that are Christ's, as has been said above, and as Paul asserts in Gal. 2:20 when he says, "And the life I now live in the flesh I live by faith in the Son of God." Although the Christian is thus free from all works, he ought in his liberty to empty himself, take upon himself the form of a servant, be made in the likeness of men, be found in human form, and to serve, help, and in every way deal with his neighbor as he sees that God through Christ has dealt and still deals with him. This he should do freely, having regard for nothing but divine approval.

THE CLOUD OF UNKNOWING

Translated by Ira Progoff
Chapter XXXI

1. After you have reached the point where you feel that you have done what is required of you according to the judgement of the Holy Church, you shall begin intently to carry out this work. Then if you find that particular acts which you have done in the past constantly come into your memory and come between you and your God, or that any new thoughts or stirring of sin does so, then you must steadfastly step above them with a fervent stirring of love and tread them down beneath your feet.

2. Try to cover over those thoughts with a thick *cloud of forgetting* as though they had never existed either for you or for any other man. And if they continue to arise, continue to put them down. As often as they come up, so often must you put them down. And if you think that the labor is great, then you may seek to develop special ways, tricks, private techniques, and spiritual devices by means of which you can put them away. And it is best to learn these methods from God by your own experience rather than from any man in this life.

From Chapter XXXII

1. Although this is so, I will tell you what seems to me to be the best of these special ways. Test them and improve upon them if you can.

2. Try as much as you can to behave as though you are not aware that these thoughts are pressing so strongly upon you between you and your God. Try to look, as it were, over their shoulders, as though you were looking for some-

thing else; and this other thing is God enclosed in a *cloud of unknowing*. If you do this, I believe that in a short time your labor will be greatly eased. I believe that when this method is correctly understood and practiced it involves nothing else than a longing desire for God, to feel Him and to see Him as much as is possible in this life. Such a desire is charity, and it always merits fulfillment.

3. There is another method, and you may test it if you wish. When you feel that you are altogether unable to press down your thoughts, cower beneath them cringing as a coward overcome in battle. Think then that it is foolishness for you to strive any longer with them, and yield yourself therefore to God in the hands of your enemies. Regard yourself then as one who has been lost forever.

4. Take the greatest care in using this method, however, for it seems to me in applying it you can melt all things to water. But when this method is correctly conceived it becomes nothing else than a true knowledge and feeling of yourself as you are, a wretched and filthy thing far worse than nothing. This knowledge and feeling is meekness. And this meekness results in God Himself coming down with great strength to avenge you on your enemies, to raise you up and with loving care dry your spiritual eyes, as the father does to his child about to perish at the mouths of wild beasts.

THE CHRISTIAN'S SECRET OF A HAPPY LIFE
Hannah Whitall Smith

I feel sure that to each one of you have come some divine intimations or foreshadowings of the life I here describe.

Have you not begun to feel dimly conscious of the voice of God speaking to you, in the depths of your soul, about these things? Has it not been a pain and a distress to you of late to discover how full your lives are of self? Has not your soul been plunged into inward trouble and doubt about certain dispositions of pursuits in which you have been formerly accustomed to indulge? Have you not begun to feel uneasy with some of your habits of life, and to wish that you could do differently in certain respects? Have not paths of devotedness and of service begun to open out before you, with the longing thought, "Oh that I could walk in them!" All these questions and doubts and this inward yearning are the voice of the Good Shepherd in your heart, seeking to call you out of that which is contrary to His will. Let me entreat of you not to turn away from His gentle pleadings! You little know the sweet paths into which He means to lead you by these very steps, nor the wonderful stores of blessedness that lie at their end, or you would spring forward with an eager joy to yield to every one of His requirements. The heights of Christian perfection can only be reached by each moment faithfully following the Guide who is to lead you there; and He reveals the way to us one step at a time, in the little things of our daily lives, asking only on our part that we yield ourselves up to His guidance. Be perfectly pliable then in His dear hands, to go where He entices you, and to turn away from all from which He makes you shrink. Obey Him perfectly the moment you are sure of His will; and you will soon find that He is leading you swiftly and easily into such a wonderful life of conformity to Himself that it will be a testimony to all around you, beyond what you yourself will ever know.

THEOLOGIA GERMANICA
THREE STAGES BY WHICH A MAN IS LED
UPWARDS UNTIL HE ATTAINETH TRUE
PERFECTION

Edited by Thomas S. Kepler

Now be assured that no one can be enlightened unless he be
first cleansed or purified and stripped. So also, no one can
be united with God unless he be first enlightened. Thus there
are three stages: first, the purification; secondly, the enlightening; thirdly, the union. The purification concerneth
those who are beginning or repenting, and is brought to pass
in a threefold wise; by contrition and sorrow for sin, by full
confession, by hearty amendment. The enlightening belongeth to such as are growing, and also taketh place in
three ways: to wit, by the eschewal of sin, by the practice of
virtue and good works, and by the willing endurance of all
manner of temptation and trials. The union belongeth to
such as are perfect, and also is brought to pass in three
ways: to wit, by pureness and singleness of heart, by love,
and by the contemplation of God, the Creator of all things.

Nothing Burneth in Hell but Self-Will

Some may say: "Now since God willeth and desireth and
doth the best that may be to everyone, He ought so to help
each man and order things for him, that they should fall out
according to his will and fulfill his desires, so that one might
be a Pope, another a Bishop, and so forth." Be assured, he
that helpeth a man to his own will, helpeth him to the worst
that he can. For the more a man followeth after his own

self-will, and self-will groweth in him, the farther off is he from God, the true Good (for nothing burneth in hell but self-will. Therefore it hath been said, "Put off thine own will, and there will be no hell"). Now God is very willing to help a man and bring him to that which is best in itself, and is of all things the best for man. But to this end, all self-will must depart, as we have said. And God would fain give man his help and counsel thereunto, for so long as a man is seeking his own good, he does not seek what is best for him, and will never find it. For a man's highest good will be and truly is, that he should not seek himself nor his own things, nor be his own end in any respect, either in things spiritual or things natural but should seek only the praise and glory of God and His holy will. This doth God teach and admonish us.

JOURNAL

John Woolman

The increase of business became my burden; for though my natural inclination was toward merchandise, yet I believed truth required me to live more free from outward cumbers; and there was now a strife in my mind between the two. In this exercise my prayers were put up to the Lord, who graciously heard me, and gave me a heart resigned to his Holy will. Then I lessened my outward business, and, as I had opportunity, told my customers of my intentions, that they might consider what shop to turn to; and in a while I wholly laid down merchandise, and followed my trade as a tailor by myself, having no apprentice. I also had a nursery of apple-trees, in which I employed some of my time in hoeing, grafting, trimming and inoculating. In merchandise it is the custom where I lived to sell chiefly on credit, and poor people often get in debt, when payment is expected, not having wherewith to pay, their creditors often sue for it at law. Having frequently observed occurrence of this kind, I found it good for me to advise poor people to take such goods as were most useful, and not costly.

.   .   .   .

About this time, a person of some distance lying sick, his brother came to me to write his will. I knew he had slaves and asking his brother, was told he intended to leave them as slaves to his children. As writing is a profitable employ, and offending sober people was disagreeable to my inclination, I was straightened in my mind; but as I looked to the Lord, he inclined my heart to his testimony; and I told the man that I believed the practice of continuing slavery to this people was not right; and had a scruple in my mind against doing writing of that kind; that though many in our society kept them as slaves, still I was not easy to be concerned in it; and desired to be excused from going to write the will. I spake to him in the fear of the Lord; and he made no reply to what I said, but went away; he also had some concerns in the practice; and I thought he was displeased with me. In this case, I had a fresh confirmation, that acting contrary to present outward interest, from a motive of Divine love, and in regard to truth and righteousness, and thereby incurring the resentment of people, opens the way to a treasure which is better than silver, and to a friendship exceeding the friendship of men.

SERMONS ON THE CATECHISM
AND LEAD US NOT INTO TEMPTATION
Martin Luther

"Into evil enticement." This is very fine old German. We say "trial," "temptation." Here we need to know what these words mean. Sins cling to us. The first temptation is that of the flesh, which says: Go ahead and have illicit intercourse with another's wife, daughter, maid! That is Master Flesh. Or he says: I am going to sell the grain, beer, or goods as dearly as I can. This is the temptation of the flesh. Here the greed of your flesh is seeking its own advantage. Then you should pray "Guard us, dear Lord, from temptation!" Likewise, the flesh seeks to satisfy its lust in glutting, guzzling, and loafing.

Next is the world, which tempts you with envy, hatred, and pride. Your neighbor irritates you to anger when you are making a bargain and all of a sudden there is impatience, the nature of the world—up she goes, blow your top, and it's all off! Then one conforms to the world. These are worldly temptations. Therefore pray: O Lord, bring it to pass that the flesh and the world shall not seduce me! Both of them, the flesh and the world, contribute much toward your feeling, in inclination to spite and lechery and dislike for your neighbor. Against all this pray: "Lead us not into temptation." Dear Father, let me not fall into this or other temptations.

The third companion and Tempter is Master Devil. He tempts you by causing you to disregard God's Word: Oh, I have to look after the beer and the malt, I can't go to hear a sermon; or if you do come to church to hear the sermon, you go to sleep, you don't take it in, you have no delight, no love, no reverence for the Word. Then pray that you may not despise it! Then, too, it is Satan's temptation when you are assailed by unbelief, diffidence, by fanatics, superstition, witchcraft, and the like. When you feel such temptations, go running to the Lord's Prayer! You have the promise that God will deliver you from the temptation of the flesh, the world, and the devil. Our whole life is nothing but temptation by these three, the flesh, the world and the devil. Therefore pray: Father, let our flesh not seduce us, let not the world deceive us, let not the devil cast us down. Thus these six petitions deal with very great matters and needs. Whatever needs are in the world, they are included in the Lord's Prayer. And all the prayers in the Psalms and all the prayers which could ever be devised are in the Lord's Prayer.

6

REVIEWS OF
FORTY-TWO CLASSICS
OF THE
SPIRITUAL LIFE
AND BIOGRAPHIES
OF THE AUTHORS

Why Particular Books and Authors
Have Been Selected for This Manual

Several criteria have been used in the selections.

I have included those authors and books which reveal a religious relationship with the Presence *and* a concern which, more often than not, has resulted in a mission to the needs of others. In general, the books I have selected fall into three divisions: (1) spiritual autobiographies, such as the journals of George Fox, John Wesley, and John Woolman; (2) devotional manuals such as *Private Devotions* by John Donne and *A Serious Call to a Devout and Holy Life* by William Law; and (3) works of mystical theology such as *Christian Perfection* by William Law and *The Scale of Perfection* by Walter Hilton.

I have excluded, on principle, the authors of general religiosity (for example, books by Kahlil Gibran), works which are doctrinally oriented (Fulton Sheen and William Barclay), works stressing the Social Gospel (Walter Rauschenbusch), books of the peace-of-mind approach (Norman Vincent Peale), and works of general sweetness and light. I have omitted these, although they may have great merit for other situations, because they did not fit the mystical provinces of the Presence with which I have dealt in this volume.

I have used one other criterion. Each of the authors has a touch of mysticism in his or her experience. By "mysticism" I mean the belief that spiritual truth and knowledge of God can be gained through personal insight instead of through logic. Most of the books have this characteristic and orientation. They have been written by Christians who believe that the heart can understand in a moment of insight what the mind may not be able to comprehend through reason. For example, Christians who have testified to such a mystical awareness are St. Augustine, Bernard of Clairvaux, Meister Eckhart, Teresa of Avila, Francis of Assisi, and John of the Cross. All have believed that the spiritual life is possible through cultivation of the Presence. There are, of course, many others who have experienced the Presence of God in this way.

To determine which others should be included, I have relied on the results of recurring public selection, as well as on the recommendations of established religious leaders.

As the years, or even centuries, pass, the general reading public seems to have a way of sorting out those testimonies of spiritual life which really contribute to religious understanding. People use and recommend for the next generation those books which prove to be the most dependable and helpful.

For example, Ignatius Loyola acknowledged the importance of the *Imitation of Christ* by depending upon it for the development of his *Spiritual Exercises*. Martin Luther praised *Theologia Germanica* by saying that, next to the Bible, "no book ever came into my hands from which I learnt more." John Wesley recommended two works of William Law as being influential in his life, *Christian Perfection* and *A Serious Call to a Devout and Holy Life*. Evelyn Underhill relied on Jean-Pierre de Caussade's *Abandonment to Divine Providence* and also looked to Baron Friedrich von Hügel, the writer of *Selected Letters*, for spiritual counsel. Dag Hammarskjöld, former Secretary-General of the United Nations, revealed in his meaningful *Markings* that he was indebted to Meister Eckhart and St. John of the Cross.

Out of the long list of accounts of the Presence, twelve

books continue to make the "most-wanted" group year after year. In order of their preference by the public, they are:

1. *Imitation of Christ* attrib. to Thomas à Kempis
2. *Confessions* by St. Augustine
3. *Little Flowers of St. Francis* by unknown editors
4. *Journal* by John Woolman
5. *The Practice of the Presence of God* by Brother Lawrence
6. *Introduction to a Devout Life* by Francis de Sales
7. *Theologia Germanica* by an unknown author
8. *Journal of George Fox* by George Fox
9. *Pilgrim's Progress* by John Bunyan
10. *A Plain Account of Christian Perfection* by John Wesley
11. *Spiritual Exercises* by Ignatius Loyola
12. *The Rule and Exercises of Holy Living* by Jeremy Taylor

Although the person who is seeking to cultivate the Presence might do well with any of these, there are two which I would recommend as starters.

Introduction to a Devout Life, by Francis de Sales, was written with the everyday person in mind. It presents the viewpoint that a new interior life is possible without the aid of the cloister. It is, therefore, a good book for those just getting into the spiritual life. It is understandable and practical.

Imitation of Christ, written, possibly, by Thomas à Kempis, has been a steady and dependable guide since the fifteenth century. It is true that it does emphasize the matter of self-renunication as well as lack of concern for the world around us. But, on the other hand, it lifts up the reality of the spiritual life so well that it cannot be overlooked.

In the following pages, I review more than forty of the best-known spiritual-life and devotional classics of Christian literature, and offer brief biographical sketches of the authors.

Book Reviews

By Unknown Authors

Lancelot Andrewes was born in Barking, England, in 1555. He was a very brilliant child who grew up in the household of a sea-captain. His early excellence at school opened many educational advantages for him as well as the chance for a career in the Church of England. His rise from the ranks was rapid as he became dean of Westminster School, bishop of Winchester, and later privy councillor and confidant of King James I.

Andrewes's ability to master fifteen languages was one of the reasons why he was chosen to help translate the Authorized (King James) Version of the Bible. He was a celebrated speaker as well as a man of deep personal piety. As such, he was a natural choice to preach the funeral sermon of Queen Elizabeth I.

Andrewes's greatest work was his *Private Prayers,* though they were originally written only for his own use. It is said that the original volume (now lost) was stained with his tears over his struggles with the behind-the-scenes issues of intrigue in the English court.

Andrewes died a bachelor in 1626.

THE PRIVATE PRAYERS OF LANCELOT ANDREWES
Lancelot Andrewes   1648

As the title implies, these are personal prayers. They were not written for publication. They were an important part of the religious devotion of Lancelot Andrewes, who was a highly educated and spiritual official of the Church of England, and a celebrated preacher.

The first part of the collection includes prayers of confession and intercession which might be used on each day of the week, over and over again. The second half are prayers for special conditions of the soul such as pleading, thanksgiving, and adoration.

The beauty of the language is notable. Almost every sentence reflects Holy Scripture, or is drawn from some religious author, or is brought down from ancient liturgies.

Because of the quality and excellence of this devotional manual, it continues to receive wide public acceptance.

Aurelius Augustine was born in Numidia, North Africa, in 354. His early life was deeply influenced by his mother, who was a Christian, certainly a minority belief at the time. He had an exceptionally keen mind, so that by the age of nineteen he was studying many different philosophies. At the same time, he admits that he lived a wild and dissolute life. In his mid-twenties he became a teacher who was known for his ability to make philosophy and literature interesting to students.

In these years, Augustine began to read Cicero's *Hortensius,* which raised a great curiosity in him, as well as doubt, about the values of his own life. The call to asceticism conflicted with his youthful passions. In the search which followed, Augustine passed through several philosophical stages of belief. Finding what he thought were weaknesses in them all, he turned to Christianity when he was thirty-three. On Easter day, in 387, he was baptized.

Augustine became a priest in 392. With the mind of a genius, he moved into leadership rapidly and was appointed bishop of Hippo at the age of forty-two. In the succeeding years, he became an outstanding "apologist" for the developing Christian Church. He died in 430. He continues to be among the most influential Christian thinkers since St. Paul.

CONFESSIONS
St. Augustine 391–401

St. Augustine has been described as one of the "profoundest intellectual geniuses of human history." His writings have influenced, directly or indirectly, every person living in the Western world. His power with words, his depth of sensuality, and his intellectual perception make him required reading.

The *Confessions* is among his most important works. Most of it is autobiographical. However, it is not an account of his deeds and misdeeds but is, rather, an acknowledgment of the Presence of God. He describes his early years, his battles with his passions, his search for truth, and his conversion from intellectual variety to Christian faith. He selects facts out of his life to illuminate his theological observations about the journey of the soul. The inquiring mind will identify with his struggle of body and spirit and will be encouraged and helped by his solutions.

This book is not easy to read but it is richly rewarding. It is one of the great books (next to the Bible) with which every Christian should be familiar. To get the most out of the *Confessions,* it should be *studied* with a good teacher.

John Baillie was born in Gairloch, Scotland, in 1886. His father was a Free Church minister who died when John was five years old. He grew up with several brothers in a strict and independent Calvinist home. His mother saw to it that he received a good education.

Early in life, Baillie turned to teaching and later became a professor at several theological schools, including Union (of New York) in the United States. Later, he returned to Scotland, where he spent twenty years as a spiritual counselor, author, lecturer, teacher, and official of the Church of Scotland.

Among Baillie's many interests was the religious Iona Community on the island off the coast of Scotland, and the world ecumenical movement. With the outbreak of war in Europe in 1939, he plunged into relief efforts and did refugee work when Germany collapsed. Because of his wide church contacts, he was instrumental in reestablishing the life of the churches on the Continent after the war.

Baillie was an extremely energetic cleric. He often participated in planning meetings for church union. He was co-president of the World Council of Churches in 1954. He died in 1956.

Among his writings are *Christian Devotion, Addresses,* and *A Diary of Private Prayer.*

A DIARY OF PRIVATE PRAYER
John Baillie   1949

In a period when all sorts of daily devotional readings flood our bookstores, this collection of thirty morning and thirty evening prayers is noteworthy because of its excellent quality. The prayers have been written for private use by this brilliant churchman and pastor of Scotland.

John Baillie's prayers stress personal righteousness as well as social concern. They often quote the Bible. They are in everyday language. They are God-oriented. They speak to the heart of the baker, businessman, or coal miner. They are calls for more integrity, honesty, purpose, and glory for everyday living in the Presence of God.

Baillie writes in plain, nontheological, up-to-date language. He testifies for the Spirit to every person and every age, old or young. He expresses a personal relationship with God that is inspiring. This book is a good example of devotional literature. It is an excellent book for those beginning to cultivate the Presence.

A DIARY OF READINGS
John Baillie   1930

The subtitle describes this book well: "Being an Anthology of Pages Suited to Engage Serious Thought. One for Every Day of the Year. Gathered from the Wisdom of Many Centuries."

John Baillie, the renowned Scottish cleric, accumulated

these selections for his own personal devotional use. His collection includes a wide variety of authors such as John Donne, Phillips Brooks, Friedrich von Hügel, William Cowper, Samuel Johnson, Izaak Walton, Albert Schweitzer, John Bunyan, and Søren Kierkegaard.

As would be expected, the 365 readings cover a broad spectrum: "better personal conduct," "the importance of resolutions," "the need of vigilance," "spiritual equilibrium," "eternity," "the inward tribunal," "the control of imagination," and "personal relationship to God."

This book has been a popular daily-reader for generations. Everyone can benefit from Baillie's selections. They are inspirational, reasonable, sound, constructive, and religious.

During the flowering of mysticism in Europe, *Jacob Boehme* was born in Gorlitz, Germany, in 1575. In his early life, he received very little education. He worked as a shepherd but, being unable to withstand the harsh outdoor life, he eventually learned the trade of a shoemaker. He became the father of six children and was known as a responsible man, but some saw him as an idealistic visionary who testified to many strange religious visions and mystical experiences.

His writings are often difficult, if not impossible, to understand—due, in part, to his lack of education as well as the depth of his mysticism. Although he continued loyal to the Catholic Church and helped in the formation of many lay-fellowship groups such as the Brethren of the Common

Life in Holland, nevertheless, toward the end of his days he was savagely attacked as a religious heretic, so that he was even in disrepute in his own city.

Evelyn Underhill says that Boehme "is among the most original of the great Christian mystics" and adds, "Boehme's mind and heart combine to give him a foremost place among the classic writers."

After a career filled with many esoteric visions which brought him inward peace and joy in spite of his detractors, Jacob Boehme died in 1624. His writings, including the *Confessions*, were posthumously published.

THE CONFESSIONS OF JACOB BOEHME
Jacob Boehme   ca.1600

These *Confessions* are a personal account of Boehme's dramatic struggle with the Devil and with God. The book often urges the reader to benefit from Boehme's inner spiritual battle, to repent and enjoy peace with Christ.

It describes Boehme's religious experiences in esoteric, symbolic ways. For example, it speaks of the dark world (unregenerate nature) and the light world (grace). It describes "the living running fire," which is Boehme's own spirit. Many meanings are hidden in a haze of inconsistent symbols. It often repeats itself. But for all of this, there is a Presence about Boehme which lifts his strange writing far above that of the average inspirational author. He relies more on the urgency of his personal experience than on rational argument. He passionately urges others to accept the life of the Spirit.

The *Confessions,* edited as a spiritual autobiography by

W. Scott Palmer, with an introduction by Evelyn Underhill, is recommended.

Dietrich Bonhoeffer, pastor, professor, patriot, family man, and martyr, was born in Breslau (then a part of Germany) in 1906. He was the son of a prominent German psychiatrist and a grandson of a professor of church history who was also a leader in the Lutheran Church. In such circumstances, Dietrich was given an excellent education, which moved him into academic life.

He served on the faculty of the University of Berlin from 1930 to 1936, when he was expelled by the growing Nazi military power, which felt he was unsympathetic to its policies.

In 1937, Bonhoeffer published *The Cost of Discipleship* and continued to speak out against the Nazis. In 1939 he moved to the United States to become Professor of Theology at Union Seminary in New York. This change was short-lived, however, as Bonhoeffer became more and more aware of the threat of the Nazis to exterminate and change much of the German culture and the Christian church. So, at great personal risk, Bonhoeffer returned to Germany to be with his family, his friends, and his church. Soon he was working actively for the overthrow of the Hitler regime.

In 1943, he was caught in a plot to bring down the Führer. He was imprisoned. It was during these years that the correspondence developed which was later collected and published under the title *Letters and Papers from Prison.* He was shot by the Gestapo just a few days before the collapse of Germany in 1945.

Bonhoeffer is recognized throughout the Christian world as an important theologian and, of course, a martyr for Christ in the twentieth century.

LIFE TOGETHER
Dietrich Bonhoeffer 1938

There are three notable books by Dietrich Bonhoeffer: *The Cost of Discipleship, Life Together,* and *Letters and Papers from Prison.* All are being claimed as classics of Christian literature because of their impact upon Christians everywhere.

Life Together was written by Bonhoeffer when he was in charge of an underground seminary in anti-church prewar Germany. It has a deeply spiritual appeal for the formation of genuine Christian communities of all kinds: family, group, church, and organization. While many write about the need for more Christian piety, and while there is continuous discussion about Christian social concern, *Life Together* introduces a new emphasis when it suggests that people dwelling "together in unity" (Psalm 133:1) are not just an ideal but a divine reality.

Bonhoeffer says: "Christian brotherhood is not an ideal which we must realize: it is rather a reality created by God in Christ in which we may participate." He then speaks of four ways of creating such communities: (1) by Sharing the Day with Others through Scripture reading, song and prayer, each being a source of joy and grace upon community; (2) by using the Day Alone for solitude and silence, meditation and intercession, each being a way to create self; (3) by Ministry to others through better listening and the bearing of others' burdens; and (4) by Confession and

Communion, in which he offers new insights to the importance of confession as a way of breaking through to Christian community.

This is an excellent spiritual-life resource for the beginner as well as the advanced Christian.

John Bunyan (sometimes spelled Bunion, Banyon, Binyan, Buignon—the family name has thirty different spellings) was born in Elstow, England, in 1628. He was the son of an unskilled repairman. Without any formal education as a youth, he enlisted in the Parliamentary Army during the Civil War against Charles I. His experiences there turned his mind toward religion, and a family. When he married, he was so poor that he described his wife and himself as "poor as poor can be, without so much household stuff as a dish or spoon." In this marriage to a deeply religious woman, he joined a nonconformist church in Bedford and later became its preacher.

By the English Acts of Restoration, preaching in those days could be done only by recognized, licensed clergy, but Bunyan, who felt called to preach, spoke anyway in whatever barns or fields would hold his listeners. He was arrested (for the first time in 1660) and spent most of the next twelve years in prison, making shoelaces to support his children. While in prison he wrote the most famous allegory in the English language, *Pilgrim's Progress*.

After his release from prison in 1672, he became more popular than ever before. He preached and wrote continuously. In fact, he published four books during his last year of life, 1688.

GRACE ABOUNDING TO THE CHIEF OF SINNERS
John Bunyan   1666

This book records John Bunyan's early spiritual struggles from childhood through his first years of preaching to the age of thirty-seven, but it is more of a spiritual exercise than an autobiography.

It was written by Bunyan while he was in prison, as encouragement to his congregation, which was facing persecution without him.

In a plain and simple style, Bunyan says there is no salvation through adherence to church ritual. Those who are saved have their sins removed by the blood of Christ. He repeats this theme over and over by telling of his own repeated spiritual struggles. Indeed, the prolonged repetition may be the book's major flaw.

The volume ends with "A Brief Account of the Author's Call to the Work of the Ministry" and "A Brief Account of the Author's Imprisonment." In general, this is a book that is more helpful as an introduction to the religious convictions of John Bunyan, than as a devotional guide.

PILGRIM'S PROGRESS
John Bunyan   1670

This highly entertaining and morally instructive allegory was written during one of Bunyan's imprisonments (for preaching without a license, but really for being a critic of the established Church of England).

The book is in two sections. The first part, reflecting Bunyan's personal conversion pilgrimage, tells of the journey of Christian from the City of Destruction to salvation in the Celestial City. Early in his trials, Christian loses his burden of sin. In spite of this, the spiritual path becomes increasingly difficult and he meets with greater obstacles. Only with the continuing aid of Hopeful is he finally able to pass through the last river and enter the gate of the City.

The second part, written ten years later, is a similar journey (in dreams) of his wife Christiana and her children. Both stories are filled with characters such as Worldly Wiseman, Talkative, and Fearing, who meet in such places as the Town of Morality, the Slough of Despond, and the Valley of Humiliation.

This is a spiritual masterpiece! It is the most famous allegory of the English language. Every person of faith should read this spiritually stimulating book.

Out of seventeenth-century France comes another spiritual-life author who cannot be overlooked in a comprehensive survey. His name is *Jean-Pierre de Caussade*. He was born in 1675 but very little is known about his first years. He apparently grew up in southern France. Further information about his parents, his childhood, and his upbringing is missing.

He became a Jesuit novice in 1693 and an ordained priest in 1704. Most of his early life was spent as a teacher of Latin and philosophy. Later he turned to preaching and from that to several administrative posts, such as being the rector of the Jesuit college in Perpignan.

What is known about Caussade comes from the numerous letters he wrote, many of which were preserved by nuns to whom he gave spiritual advice in his various leadership capacities. Indeed, the book ascribed to him, *Abandonment to Divine Providence,* was not written by him at all. It was edited, from a collection of letters and notes on his lectures, by a French Jesuit, Father Henri Ramiere. It appeared in 1861, more than a hundred years after Caussade's death in 1751.

Although Caussade had an extremely busy life, he was greatly attracted to silence and solitude and the enjoyment of each moment as a gift from God.

ABANDONMENT TO DIVINE PROVIDENCE
Jean-Pierre de Caussade   1861

A new translator, John Beevers, states in his explanatory introduction to this short, intense, and passionately written appeal that Caussade "insists over and over again that we must live from moment to moment. The past is past, the future is yet to be. There is nothing we can do about either, but we can deal with what is happening from moment to moment. We must realize there is nothing at all which happens unless willed by God and our all important duty is to cooperate with that will."

Two key sentences by Caussade will also help in understanding his idea: (1) "If we have abandoned ourselves to God, there is only one rule for us: the duty of the present moment." (2) "The events of each moment are stamped with the will of God . . . .we find all that is necessary in the present moment. It is the trivialities of life—as we consider them—which would do marvels for us if only we did not despise them."

The book demands careful reading and much reflection. It is not recommended for the novice.

In unusual and beautiful style, Izaak Walton wrote a short biography of *John Donne,* as an introduction to *Devotions upon Emergent Occasions.* He began: "Master John Donne was born in London, in the year 1573, of good and virtuous parents; and through his own learning and other multiplied merits, may justly appear sufficient to dignify both himself and his posterity."

As a youth, Donne received tutoring and training commensurate with the high estate of his birth. (His mother was a descendant of Sir Thomas More, the famous Lord Chancellor of England in the reign of Henry VIII.)

As a young man, Donne traveled a good deal and moved handsomely among the high circles of politics and society. He studied law; considered many possible court appointments; wrote poetry which was later regarded, along with Milton's, as the best in the English language; was a confidant of King James; and then seriously returned to a youthful interest, religion. He entered the Church of England with high honors. The same summer that he took his sacred vows, he was made the King's Chaplain. Later he became dean of St. Paul's Cathedral and attracted large congregations with his powerful oratory.

In his fifty-fourth year, John Donne became ill with consumption. Upon his recovery, he published *Devotions upon Emergent Occasions,* which Walton describes as "a composition of meditations, disquisitions, and prayers he wrote on his sick bed." He died a few years later, in 1631.

DEVOTIONS UPON EMERGENT OCCASIONS
John Donne   1630

This diary of sickness, doctor's advice, and cure, is called *Devotions* because Donne interprets the whole personal affair of his life as being in the hands of God.

The account is divided into twenty-three parts, each representing a stage in his affliction. For example, he tells of "The first grudging of the sickness," "The patient takes his bed," "The king sends his own physician," "I sleep not day or night," and how "From the bells of the church adjoining, I am daily remembered of my burial in the funerals of others." He reports that the doctors "Proceed to purge" and how "God prospers their practice."

Devotions is a book of witty and thoughtful comments on the meaning of sickness. It is introspective and metaphysical, but to read it solely with this perspective would be to miss its theological flavor. If the reader can overlook the seventeenth-century unscientific references, he will find this an unusual devotional. However, it is not a popular one.

Meister Eckhart was one of the leaders of the German age of mysticism in the thirteenth and fourteenth centuries. All we know of his early life comes from juiceless church records.

He was born in 1260. His father was a steward in a knight's castle. At about the age of fifteen, he entered the Dominican monastery at Erfurt. Apparently he studied well, for he quickly rose in responsibility. In 1300, he was sent on a teaching mission to Paris where he attracted much attention because of his religious enthusiasm. It seemed the beginning of a rapid rise in the power-structure of the Church.

However, after a few years, Eckhart came into conflict with the established religious ideas of the time because he opposed fasting, vigils, or asceticism as marks of salvation. He felt "the soul of man is the spark of God." He was convinced that, though the rituals of the Church were of some value, the real springs of religious life lay far deeper in the mystical experience.

As he moved further and further into mysticism, his official Church leadership became more and more jeopardized. By 1327, he was charged with heresy and was in the midst of being brought to trial when he died in 1328. Pope John XXII condemned him posthumously a year later.

Eckhart's influence continued, however, through the Friends of God, a movement for aiding the poor and uneducated, which he had previously helped organize in the Low Countries.

MEISTER ECKHART
Translated by Raymond Blakney   1300

Meister Eckhart's symbolic and mystical language is not always easy to understand today. He was a man with one idea, the unity of the human and the divine. He understood the relationship to be a mystical one. "God never tied Man's salvation to any pattern of life."

The book contains twenty-eight sermons, most of which have been reconstructed from Eckhart's notes, or notes of his congregations. It includes "The Talks of Instruction," which is practical advice on the religious problems of life. Another section of the volume contains Eckhart's "Book of Divine Comfort," in which the mystic deals with suffering and evil. The translation also presents, for the first time in English, Eckhart's planned defense against the Church's charge of heresy and too much mysticism, a condemnation he was preparing to refute when he died.

This book is a good introduction to the leader of the flowering of mysticism. It provides good background material for the understanding of the mystical aspect of the Presence of God. It is, however, of more value for its historical insight than for its use as a devotional guide.

François Fénelon was born of wealthy parents in a luxurious French castle in 1651. He was raised to be pious and was educated in classical literature and languages. He proved to have a very keen mind.

Fénelon became a priest in 1675. He attracted attention as an excellent teacher and was chosen to tutor the grandson of King Louis XIV. The entire court praised his accomplishments.

The life at the court in those days was one of intrigue and corruption. In the face of this, Fénelon gathered a small group of friends who sought to live simply and spiritually. He corresponded a great deal and acted as spiritual counselor to many. It is out of these letters that his book *Christian Perfection* is edited.

Fénelon championed the writings of Mme Guyon, who was later condemned by the Church as a Quietist, that is, a passive and nonproductive contemplative. He lost favor at the court over this issue in spite of the fact that his own talents in politics, literature, and theology were outstanding.

Fénelon combined faith and works dramatically when his diocese was invaded and destroyed by enemy soldiers from Spain in 1709. He turned his family's palace into a hospital for the wounded and shared his inherited wealth with the government, to buy food to relieve the ensuing famine.

He died in 1715, ending a life as a well-known director of souls.

CHRISTIAN PERFECTION
François Fénelon   1700

This is a collection of meditations taken from letters that Fénelon wrote while he was tutor and priest at the French court.

The reflections cover a wide range of topics in sensible, practical, God-oriented ways.

The book is divided into two sections. The first part (chapters 1 to 28) consists of essays which call readers to the moral Christian life, as Fénelon discusses such topics as "The Use of Time," "True Liberty," "Dryness and Distractions," "Helps in Sadness," "Interior Peace," and "Special Friendships."

The second part (chapters 29 to 41) deals in longer fashion with some of the salient issues of the Christian faith, such as "Knowing God," "The Word Within," "Suffering," and the "Reality of Pure Love."

The central theme underlying all that Fénelon believes is the Providence of God: "Let God act. He will show the way."

Fénelon writes with an Emerson-like reasonableness. He is provocative and refreshing. He raises questions about the timeless spiritual values which affect the lives of all men and women. He is an attractive and stimulating writer who should be read by people of the twentieth century.

A GUIDE TO TRUE PEACE
Fénelon—Guyon—Molinos   ca. 1813

This pocket-sized book is compiled from the writings of François Fénelon, Mme Jeanne de la Motte Guyon, and Miguel de Molinos, who lived in France and Italy in the eighteenth century. It was originally published in America in 1813. It has been used as a devotional book by members of the Society of Friends. It has been reedited by Howard H. Brinton.

Always printed in pocket-size, the book is compiled as an aid to interior development and a resource of prayer in the midst of worldly difficulties. The book is a collection of three short monographs: *Short Method of Prayer* by Mme Guyon, *Maxims of the Saints* by Fénelon, and *Spiritual Guide* by Molinos.

The theme of the book is that, in order to control our outward natures, we must first learn to master our inward selves; "there is no real peace in society until there is peace within."

The guide deals with such matters as spiritual dryness, self-denial, prayer, temptations, and tribulations.

It should be recalled that both Mme Guyon and Molinos lost favor with the Church in their day. They were charged with heresy for being Quietists, which many felt was a passive withdrawal into irresponsibility. The book should be read with this background in mind, but it is personally helpful, nonetheless.

George Fox was born into a family of poor English weavers in 1624. After a sparse education, he began a trade as a shoemaker. However, when he was nineteen, he found it necessary to separate himself from his friends, because he disapproved of their "worldly ways," notably drinking. Others bothered his growing religious sensitivity, especially the "professors of religion" (clergy) who preached "nothingness."

By the time he was twenty-three, Fox was also preaching, often attracting large crowds and many well-known people, such as William Penn (later of Pennsylvania history). He spoke in "steeple houses" after the regular parish priests had ended their services. But such challenging tactics, along with fiery sermons critical of the established Church, brought him his (first) imprisonment in 1649.

Undaunted, Fox organized his followers from his prison cell with such skill that eventually they formed what has become the Society of Friends (or Quakers, as they were originally called to describe their quaking excitement during Fox's preaching). Quakers reflect Fox's belief in the guidance and healing of the Inner Light.

From 1669 to 1684, Fox traveled extensively, evangelizing Ireland, the West Indies, the United States, and Holland. He died in 1691.

JOURNAL
George Fox 1694

This spiritual autobiography is a vivid picture, drawn from everyday life, of a remarkable man: religious mystic, traveling evangelist, and inspired religious prophet. It carries the reader back into seventeenth-century England, a time in which Fox sought to be a purifying critic of the forms and rituals of the Church of England.

The book, containing papers and letters, was dictated to his stepson-in-law, Thomas Lower. It is filled with accounts of trials and imprisonments, which give an excellent view of the judicial methods of the times. It reflects much of English life up to the year 1675, when it was concluded (though Fox did not die until 1691).

The *Journal* is Fox's only major piece of writing. It

stands as a repudiation of violence and offers many examples of the practical power of love. It tells of Fox's various visions and his "great openings," as well as his reliance upon the Inner Light. The work is too long for popular interest, but it is a worthy devotional resource, nonetheless.

Francis de Sales was born in the castle of a noble family in Savoy, France, about fifty miles from Geneva, in 1567. As a youth, he knew the best schools and became proficient in rhetoric and philosophy, as well as Hebrew. Although religion seems to have interested him as a young man, he appeared headed for an outstanding political career. At twenty-five years of age, he was approved as a candidate to the senate at Savoy. Power and position awaited him, as well as a new wife, likewise from nobility, chosen for him by his father. But it was all too well planned, apparently, for Francis. A violent conflict with his father caused him to break away from being directed by others and he returned to his youthful interest, the Church. He entered the priesthood, later being ordained in 1593.

At first, Francis preached and visited the poor. But as he continued in the Church, he became more and more involved in theology as well as administration. He was an excellent preacher and was willing to engage in controversy in the hope of winning converts. "I will draw them by the bonds of Adam, by the bonds of love," he said.

In 1602, Francis became bishop of Geneva, having built his career upon expressing his faith in service, and having founded the Visitation Order, for the care of the sick.

He wrote two devotional masterpieces: *Introduction to a Devout Life,* a book of devotion and spiritual consolation; and *The Treatise on the Love of God* for those more advanced in the Spirit.

Francis died in 1622. He was canonized by the Catholic Church in 1665.

INTRODUCTION TO A DEVOUT LIFE
Francis de Sales 1608

This has been called a "masterpiece of psychology, practical-morality and common sense." It outlines what has become known as the "Salesian" method of meditation, which is recognized as a system of spiritual direction by the Roman Catholic Church. This method encourages:

1. Preparation: think of God everywhere around you.

2. Meditation: think about improvement.

3. Resolution: decide how you can be better; be more Christ-like.

4. Thanksgiving and Prayer: how to continue with God.

The *Introduction* has remained a favorite for centuries because it helps all classes of men and women develop more devotional Christian lives even while they do the work of the world. Francis de Sales wrote for the "man in the street." He envisions a regular course of discipline which the Christian can use to grow in grace. He employs many illustrations as well as sound advice on Patience, Humility, Friendship, Temptation, and Death.

This book is an unsurpassed introduction to the devout life for every person. It is highly recommended.

Few men have had such a colorful church life as *Francis of Assisi*. Born in 1182, the son of a wealthy Italian merchant from Assisi in Italy, Francis was a popular youth, with talents, money, and social standing. As a young man he knew all of his generation's songs and dances.

During his early twenties, he spent a year as a prisoner of war (following a battle between Assisi and Perugia). A long illness and growing maturity awakened him to the poverty surrounding his life of ease and wealth. He began to attend church more often. One day, while at mass, he heard words from the crucifix which told him, "Francis, go and repair my church, which is in ruins." The extraordinary vision was a turning-point in his life. He began to organize persons who would give more of their lives for the poor.

As his interest, influence, and mission grew, Francis of Assisi appealed to Pope Innocent III for ecclesiastical endorsement and financial support. Within seven years, he had expanded the work for the poor from central Italy into Hungary, Spain, and even Syria. However, many of the clergy resisted the movement because his vows of poverty and servanthood were too stringent. Papal approval was slow.

To the end of his life, Francis aided those in poverty, established monasteries, built churches, founded hospitals, and always counseled the spiritually lonely. He died in 1226; two years later his Franciscan Order was officially recognized. It is said that "St. Francis of Assisi sparked one of the most meaningful revival movements in Christian history."

LITTLE FLOWERS OF ST. FRANCIS
Anonymous Editor   ca. 1200

This collection of stories, allegories, anecdotes, and wise conversations was created by several persons in memory of

St. Francis, about one hundred years after his death. The book was an effort to clarify the policies of the new Franciscan way of life and to authenticate the spirit of the growing Order.

The translation by Raphael Brown is recommended, not only because it makes excellent reading but also because Brown has included additional material, such as "The Life of Brother Juniper," "The Life of Brother Giles," and "The Sayings of Brother Giles."

Many of the stories and parables idealize the love of St. Francis for poverty, humility, and simplicity. If you can look beyond the medieval flavor, such as St. Francis preaching to the birds or to the fishes, you will be much rewarded with thought-provoking examples of how to live the Christian life, from a Franciscan point of dedication. This is a spiritual classic.

In the early 1930s, when ordination for women was rare, *Georgia Elma Harkness* was ordained a deacon in the Methodist Episcopal Church. Her life has always been like this progressive event.

She was born in 1891 in the northeastern part of New York, in a rural area called Harkness, which had been named for her grandfather. She grew up there, revealing an early interest in knowledge and an ability to master it.

She attended an array of colleges beginning with Cornell in New York in 1912, then Boston University, and later Harvard and Yale. At the first two, she took degrees.

Her career included teaching Latin to high-schoolers, the English Bible to college students, and religion to graduate professionals. As an ordained minister, she taught at Elmira College, Mount Holyoke College, International Christian University in Japan, Garret Theological Seminary (1940–1950), and Pacific School of Religion (1950–1961).

At the time of her death in 1974, she was working on her thirty-ninth book. They had all been about theology and related fields, her interest being to make Belief understandable to laypersons. She had published three books of poetry and five devotional manuals. Her understanding of the faith had made her United-Methodism's foremost woman theologian.

DARK NIGHT OF THE SOUL
Georgia Harkness   1945

Having taught for thirty years in many of the theological schools of the United States, Georgia Harkness is well qualified to speak about the spiritual life. In this book, she writes for the layperson who has tried, but without success, to overcome depression and the "dark night" by means of religious faith.

She begins with biblical personalities (Jeremiah and Job) as well as examples of people today who have experienced the darkness. She makes their plight understandable by explanations from theology, medicine, and psychiatry.

She patiently surveys every reason for the "dark night" experience and makes many suggestions for overcoming spiritual depression.

The last several chapters contain her thoughtful commentaries on St. John of the Cross, Mme Guyon, *Imitation of Christ,* and *The Practice of the Presence of God.*

This book is filled with lots of excellent practical counsel on moving from spiritual depression to inner renewal. It is for the conscientious seeker.

A DEVOTIONAL TREASURY
FROM THE EARLY CHURCH
Georgia Harkness   1968

Georgia Harkness, "the foremost woman Methodist theologian in the United States," has created a valuable devotional manual by gathering together a number of selections from the worship life of the early Christian Church. The excerpts pick up where the Bible leaves off. They include early Church prayers and hymns; letters of counsel from the Odes of Solomon; examples of personal Christian triumph, as in First Clement; moral injunctions, as in the Letter of Barnabas; and such memorable passages as the martyrdom of Polycarp and the description of a Christian in the Letter to Diognetus.

The material is timeless. The selections call us to the depth of faith experienced by the early Christians.

Harkness, out of much experience, has chosen excellent resources which need to be made available for more twentieth-century men and women. She has edited a resource which should be in every church library and on the shelves of most clergy.

To many of her readers, she was known as "E. Herman." To others her identity was even more camouflaged by the use of a pen name. She rarely used her first name, "Emily."

She was born in England and educated in London schools, but we know little more about her family background or childhood. Indeed, she seemed to want it that way, although later circumstances in her life thrust her into public view when she became an author and a publisher.

Emily Herman was a regular contributor to both British and American journals of religion. She was the editor of the English *Presbyterian* from 1913 until its publication was suspended because of the war.

She wrote a number of books, most of them about the spiritual life, such as *The Meaning and Value of Mysticism* in 1915, *Christianity in the New Age* in 1919, and *Creative Prayer* in 1921. She was also the author of an article on Quietism for the *Hastings Encyclopedia of Religion and Ethics*.

Little is known publicly concerning Mrs. Herman's personal life, possibly by her own design. We do know that she had such personal interests as meditative walking, writing poetry, and studying folklore. She was married to a minister of the Presbyterian Church in England.

As an author, she will long be remembered for her book called *Creative Prayer*.

CREATIVE PRAYER
Emily Herman   ca. 1930

Mrs. Herman understands that prayer is foreign to many persons, so she explains the unseen mechanisms of prayer in a practical way, offering a reasoned introduction for the beginner. She also develops sharp insights for the advanced pray-er. "Prayer is not a special romance or psychic dream," she says, "but an act of devotion influencing the very depth of soul, permeating the whole life and shaping every action.''

Herman deals with (1) the way to achieve silence, (2) the techniques of meditation, (3) the process of giving up self to God, (4) the pathway to spiritual power, (5) the logic of intercessory prayer, and (6) the meaning of offering ourselves for the sins of others.

This is sound, carefully created, spiritual counsel on the reality of prayer. It may well prove to be a new classic.

It is far from the popular religious book but, rather, deserves dedicated and faithful attention. It is a gold mine for understanding the spiritual life.

The date and place of *Walter Hilton's* birth are unknown, although the area was probably England and the time around 1330. He followed a reclusive life-style for many of his adult years and purposefully minimized any knowledge about himself.

Information which can be gathered from his Latin writings, however, suggest that he later changed his mind about being a recluse and wished to be more openly related to the regular religious life of the Church. Official records confirm that he became a Canon Regular of St. Augustine at the Priory of St. Peter at Thurgarten near Southwall. They add that he died in 1395.

Hilton's fame rests on one book, *The Scale of Perfection,* which, some say, is the most complete and balanced treatise on the interior life to come out of the Middle Ages. For centuries, the *Scale* was one of the most popular of all English spiritual books. In content, it is not unlike *The Cloud of Unknowing,* which suggests to some that Hilton may be the author of that classic. There are even those who believe that Hilton may be the author of *Imitation of Christ.*

THE SCALE OF PERFECTION
Walter Hilton   1494

This relatively little-known devotional guidebook has been retranslated and republished recently.

Walter Hilton is a lucid writer and presents his position very readably. He takes the point of view that spiritual ascent is impossible if it is not, at the same time, a moral ascent. Thus he leads the reader on a step-by-step journey of rooting out from the soul all the sins of this world and the flesh. ''Then the virtues and graces which the soul receives when its spiritual eyes are opened gives it the grace of contemplation.''

Hilton finds many contemporary seekers sympathetic to his *Scale* when he suggests that we should want the ''truth'' above everything. He is aware, however, that with the greatest of dedication, we often slip back. His depth of patient encouragement helps us renew the battle.

The translation of Leo Sherley-Price with editing by Don Illtyd Trethowan presents the work in clear format for the modern reader. It also provides an explanatory introduction. The book is more suited to the advanced religious.

Friedrich von Hügel was born into an old noble Rhineland family in Florence, Italy, in 1852. His father was the Austrian Minister to the Grand Ducal State of Tuscany. His mother was the daughter of General Francis Farguharson of Scotland.

Von Hügel never went to a school or university, but was tutored by a succession of capable educators. He became skilled in four languages: English, German, French, and Italian. He developed a lifelong interest in geology. He received spiritual development from two priests who helped him shape his life: Father Raymond Hocking and Abbé Huvelin. Under these men, von Hügel became one of the best critical scholars of the Bible in the Roman Catholic Church of his time.

Unfortunately, such an advantaged upbringing was marred by poor health, as well as long periods of spiritual doubt and darkness. In his late teen years he lost his father. A year or so afterward, he contracted typhoid fever. This left him permanently deaf, nervous, and in generally fragile health. Then spiritual problems of doubt and anxiety developed. In fact, he says it was not until he was forty that the cloud of religious uncertainty began to clear.

Von Hügel was a teacher, spiritual adviser, and author. The book by which he is best remembered is *The Mystical Element of Religion as Studied in St. Catherine of Genoa and Her Friends,* which he wrote in 1908. The *Selected Letters* was published in London in 1927, two years after Von Hügel's death.

SELECTED LETTERS
Baron Friedrich von Hügel   1927

Selected Letters covers correspondence between von Hügel and some of the most astute minds of Europe, during the years 1896 to 1924.

Inasmuch as von Hügel was always in frail health, and could give only half of each day to writing, the style of the letters reflects much forethought. In fact. his sentences were described by his closest friend, George Tyrrell, as "tight sausages."

Twenty-seven of the *Letters* are to Tyrrell, twenty-five to Maude Petre, who became Tyrrell's biographer.

The letters are concerned with the nature of God and the nature of religion. Some are to a friend, in her last illness, on the subject of suffering. They could be a classic in themselves. In letters to a niece, von Hügel gives some timeless advice on how to overcome inward dryness. Central to all of the letters is a mystical quality combined with great intellectualism, so characteristic of von Hügel.

In appraising von Hügel, Maude Petre said that "he was one who had done more than any man living to bring together the profoundest religious thinkers of the age." Such a commendation ought to encourage everyone to become familiar with the *Selected Letters,* and the spiritual counsel of von Hügel.

John of the Cross (born *John de Yepes*) was one of the famous Christian mystics. He was born in Spain in 1542 and grew up in a poor family. He obtained a good education and sought to train for the life of a priest. Through great personal desire and determination, he entered the Order of Carmelites in 1563.

It was only a few years later that he met the woman who was to change his life, Teresa of Avila. Teresa was engaged in bringing about disciplinary reforms within the Order. She encouraged him to support the effort and, in 1586, changing his name to Brother John of the Cross, he became part of the reform movement. It was a decision to be freighted with trials and obstacles.

Those who were opposed to reform seized John several years later and put him in solitary prison for nine months. He escaped and pressed the idea of reform all the more strenuously, with the result that the last years of his life were embroiled in bitter controversy. Humiliated because his opponents denied him positions of influence, which he felt important to his reforms, he died in 1591.

John's chief writings are *Ascent of Mount Carmel,* which is "an orderly treatise on the development of the spiritual life intended for the use of those who have the care of souls," and *Dark Night of the Soul,* an intermingling of philosophy and mystical theology.

DARK NIGHT OF THE SOUL
John of the Cross   ca. 1587

This is a classic presentation of contemplative, highly structured mysticism, by a consummate spiritual master, St. John of Spain. *Dark Night of the Soul* is the second part of *Ascent of Mount Carmel,* in both of which, but in deepening degrees, St. John teaches the seeker how to deny and purify oneself (with the help of grace) in order to find union with God.

St. John, who skillfully mixes philosophy and mystical theology, shows that the ascent to Mount Carmel can best be achieved by a disciplined religious life, and that the soul must pass through several periods of darkness as it seeks to throw off the attraction of the senses. He writes: "The soul must be made completely arid, if it hopes for union with God.''

St. John is the most sublime of all the Spanish mystics. He provides direction for those who are experienced in contemplation. For those who use this classic, I recommend the translation of E. Allison Peers for its clarity and readability.

Later to become one of the better-known American Quakers, *Thomas Raymond Kelly* was born on a farm in Ohio in 1893. When he was four, his father died; he grew up in a home, guided by a conscientious Quaker mother, which had few luxuries.

In school, Kelly's first interest appeared to be chemistry, which he pursued even at college; but a growing concern about people and human needs turned him away from science to theology. He entered Hartford Theological Seminary in 1916.

The coming of World War I deeply moved Kelly, for he was sensitive, by theological awareness as well as personal Quaker feelings, to human suffering. He volunteered for war relief work in the midst of the fighting in Europe. After the war, he returned to the United States and took up his career as a teacher; teaching at Pendle Hill, University of Hawaii, Earlham College, and Haverford College. During these years, he developed his ability and depth as a speaker for the Quaker cause and beliefs, and was in much demand.

Kelly never saw the spiritual life as one-sided. He had spent much of his life in caring for the suffering of others and he always balanced his emphasis upon the interior life with a concern for better social conditions.

A Testament of Devotion is his best-known book. A number of monographs and short addresses by him have also been published.

Thomas R. Kelly died in 1941.

A TESTAMENT OF DEVOTION
Thomas R. Kelly   1941

This is a collection of devotional essays and college lectures given by Thomas R. Kelly during the last three, and most productive, years of his short life. The material was published posthumously. The relatively few pages of this book (119) reveal an exceptional spirit, which can be missed by the uninitiated. The *Testament* emphasizes the continual awareness of the Presence of God, very much like the letters of Brother Lawrence: "Listen outwardly but within, behind the scenes, keep up a silent prayer."

The contents include such topics as: The Light Within, Holy Obedience, The Blessed Community, The Simplification of Life, and Social Concern.

Kelly reflects the spirit of the Quakers. He combines spiritual concern with social commitment. His *Testament* is a "must" for spiritual growth.

The first of seven children, *Søren Kierkegaard* was born in Copenhagen in 1813, into a family of wealth, his father having amassed a fortune in the wool business. The home was a meeting place for intellectuals, which stimulated Søren's gifted mind, though the child was sickly in body.

When he was twenty-two, Kierkegaard discovered that

soon after the death of his mother, his father had been obliged to marry a household servant. The shock of knowing about his father's background threw him into melancholy which affected him all the rest of his life.

Following an unhappy love affair and a broken engagement, Kierkegaard found his vocation—writing. From 1842 to 1848, he wrote prodigiously, much of his material being attacks upon the hypocrisy of the press, the established Church, and comfortable Christianity. Often he used pseudonyms, instead of his own name—nineteen in all—but most people identified the author anyway.

Kierkegaard wrote with the purpose of unsettling the reader by "revealing to him the true character of the dwelling he had inhabited."

It was not until seventy years after his death in 1855 that he really became known as a significant author outside of Denmark.

PURITY OF HEART
Søren Kierkegaard   1846

The complete title is *Purity of Heart Is to Will One Thing.* It is from James 4:8: "purify your hearts, you double-minded."

Kierkegaard says the individual must not hide behind the crowd but must be responsible for his or her individual self. Each person must stand forth as a solitary individual from whom all dross and duplicity must be removed, all hypocrisy dropped, and all evasions and escapes overcome. "Each shall render an account unto God as an individual." This theme is played upon over and over, from every angle.

The book is beautifully written: "the clouds hang as they

please and dream only of themselves.'' Its emphasis upon removing all escapes, evasions, and self-deceptions precedes Sigmund Freud, and makes the message of the book relevant to today's psychological emphasis.

The spirit of the book is rational, patient, determined, and concerned. It is not complicated reading. The author's style is conversational 'in its personal and persistent appeal to the reader to become a responsible solitary individual before God.

William Law was born in England in 1686. He was well educated as a youth and grew up in a family with high moral and ethical principles. When he was twenty-eight, while in academic life and in training for the priesthood in the Church of England, he was required to take an oath of allegiance to the new king, George I. He refused. Thereafter he was denied a future with the Church, so he spent much of his life as a writer. He is recognized as one of the outstanding English authors on practical religion, writing at a time when faith in England was at a low ebb while rationalism and skepticism were popular.

When Law's *Christian Perfection* and *A Serious Call to a Devout and Holy Life* were published in 1727 and 1728, they made him famous. *Serious Call* ranks, along with Bunyan's *Pilgrim's Progress,* as one of the most influential books for the spiritual life of the eighteenth century. Many years later, he wrote *Spirit of Prayer* (in 1750) and then *Spirit of Love* (in 1754). Both are difficult to read and often out of print because of their strong emphasis upon esoteric mysticism, into which Law had moved as a close follower of Jacob Boehme, the German mystic.

Law's earlier writings had a great influence upon John Wesley and Dr. Samuel Johnson, the English literary personality who compiled one of the first dictionaries of the English language. Johnson wrote that Law influenced his "thinking about religion in earnest." Indeed, by the spiritual power of his language, William Law continues to influence many souls for faith, although he died as long ago as 1761.

CHRISTIAN PERFECTION
William Law   1726

"The finest piece of hortatory theology in any language" was the comment about *Christian Perfection* by Dr. Samuel Johnson, famous man of letters of William Law's own day.

The work is like a collection of sermon-meditations, based upon New Testament parables and quotations. The main theme is the rejection of the pleasures and accomplishments of the world in favor of "the right performance of our necessary duties." Law argues that "the renunciation of the world is at the very heart of Christianity."

The book reflects the theology of this point of view. It contains no references to the social or political time in which it was written. It is personally devotional, with little concern for the needs of others. Law moralizes a great deal on how "our Saviour came into this world to put an end to the designs of flesh and blood."

I recommend the new more readable and modern edition of Erwin Paul Rudolph.

A SERIOUS CALL TO A DEVOUT AND HOLY LIFE
William Law   1728

This is an urgent exhortation by a well-educated, extremely dedicated priest who mingles faith with satire in order to urge well-to-do leisured persons to follow the prayerful discipline of the Christian life.

It is presented in two parts: first, a guide to serving God in the external affairs of life; second, a guide to prayer and the development of the interior spirit. In both sections the reasonableness of the devout life is stressed through examples and character sketches, as everyone is called to observe greater personal holiness: "Piety and goodness are the laws of human nature."

The work emphasizes the importance of religious observances as the pathway to finding God, but it has little concern for social reforms or improving the conditions of the times.

I suggest that you obtain a newly edited and abridged edition by John W. Meister and others, who have made *A Serious Call to a Devout and Holy Life* much more understandable for the reader of today.

Brother Lawrence (born *Nicholas Herman* in 1611) was the son of peasant parents in Lorraine, France. Of his upbringing we know nothing. About the time he was eighteen he had a conversion experience, when on a midwinter's day he observed a leafless tree. Reflection impressed him with the fact that the tree would have leaves again. The experience left him with a "high view of the presence and power of God."

At that time, the Thirty Years' War, engaging all of Europe, was being fought. Nicholas was conscripted into General Wallenstein's army on the side of the empire. During a battle he was wounded in the leg, which left him with a severe limp for the rest of his life.

Partly due to his inner-religious spirit and partly because he was ill-equipped to do anything else, he entered the Carmelite convent in Paris as a cook and lay brother in 1651. In such surroundings his religious sense deepened. He became an adviser and spiritual counselor to people of high and low estate. Important persons would travel great distances to consult with him on spiritual matters.

He wrote numerous letters of spiritual counsel. Some of these were later collected in a book called *The Practice of the Presence of God*. At the age of eighty, still serving in the kitchen, Brother Lawrence died in 1691.

THE PRACTICE OF THE PRESENCE OF GOD
Brother Lawrence   1700

This small collection of fifteen letters and four "conversations" was put together by the friends of Brother Lawrence after his death.

Through them all, Brother Lawrence speaks with clear simplicity about what prayer and the Presence meant to him—and how he found both in his everyday experiences. One of the secrets of his spirit was his complete dependence upon God. He was absolutely sure that God was present all of the time. In practicing this Presence, he developed sublime inner peace and security.

This little book has become an outstanding classic. It avoids dogma and theological argument. It stresses attentiveness to God, no matter where one is or what one is doing.

The simple beauty of this book is deceptive. Like a great work of art, it impresses us the more we study and understand it. It is one of the better devotional classics with which all pilgrims of the spiritual life should be acquainted.

Ignatius Loyola was born of a noble family in Spain, in 1490, as Inigo de Onaz y Loyola, the last of seven children. He received an excellent education and as a young man was appointed to the court of Ferdinand and Isabella. Because of his capabilities, he was given command of a small army when his country battled France in 1521. He was wounded and forced to spend much time recuperating. It was during this period of enforced reflection that he began to consider the Church. When able to do so, he undertook the life of a hermit, which brought him a tremendous inner battle concerning his life and religion. No amount of confession or fasting gave him any peace, until finally, in despair, he offered to give his whole life to God and to the Church.

Loyola's years as a student and a military person now bore fruit of a different kind. He began to organize his religious-minded friends into a disciplined movement to help and to educate the poor. The growing organization became known as the Society of Jesus. Always organizing and planning, Loyola wrote and rewrote a discipline which would ensure the dedication of the Order, *Spiritual Exercises*. The original text has been lost, or was destroyed by the author. The oldest known text is that of 1541. Pope Paul officially approved the Order of Jesuits in 1540.

When Ignatius died in 1556, more than one thousand Jesuits were working on four continents. Their religious order emphasizes good preaching, regular communion, well-managed schools, overseas missions, and the discipline of confession.

SPIRITUAL EXERCISES
Ignatius Loyola 1522

These *Exercises* have been a point of departure for most of the modern systems for the direction of the soul. They are a summary of the most profound principles of ascetical theology, i.e., one must cut the ties with all material, as well as spiritual, possessions.

At first reading, the famous *Exercises* appear to contain familiar theological ideas and overused scriptural texts. But, like a great deal of devotional material, beneath the surface lies a masterpiece of psychological and spiritual insight.

The *Exercises* are a set of disciplines which are schedules of four units of retreat (by day, week, month, or even individual ordering). They are designed to be more prayed than read.

If the Protestant will look beyond Loyola's sixteenth-century slavish attitude toward the Church, he or she will find the *Exercises* most rewarding for personal piety. For best results, however, the retreatant should have the counsel of a director.

Blaise Pascal, mathematician, religious philosopher, and scientist, was born in Clermont-Ferrand, France, in 1623.

His father took charge of his education and first taught him languages, waiting until later for the sciences. So the brilliant child taught himself geometry and had joined a mathematical academy by the time he was twelve.

In 1645, Pascal's father had an accident which confined him to the home. Among many visitors who came were some Jansenists—a Roman Catholic heresy—who held beliefs contrary to the Jesuit background of the Pascal family. Later, both Blaise and his sister were converted and joined the Jansenist convent at Port Royal. Blaise became a monk there in 1654, while continuing his scientific experiments.

When the Jansenists came under attack by the Jesuits (in 1656) because of their heretical teaching, Pascal defended them in what are known as his *Provincial Letters*—eighteen masterpieces of wit and irony.

Ill health brought Pascal's death in 1662.

Among the things Pascal left was an unfinished theological work called *Pensées,* which deals with salient points of Christian theology, such as faith versus reason. It is one of the important books of religious thought.

Pascal believed that faith is a sounder guide than reason. Reason can go far, but it has limits. Faith has no limits.

PENSÉES
Blaise Pascal   1844

When Blaise Pascal died at the age of thirty-nine, there were found among his very few possessions a great mass of notes that he had apparently been preparing with the intention of some day publishing a master defense of Christianity against atheists and agnostics. The notes were not arranged in any special order, with the result that friends and scholars have organized and reorganized the material. Thus *Pensées* is a scintillating collection of observations about Christianity by a man who was a genius in several fields, among them mathematics and science as well as religion, which enabled him to have a valuable perspective from which he studied, appraised, and wrote about Christian beliefs.

Pensées, or "Thoughts," points with recurring emphasis to the theme: in order to find the meaning of self, life, and God, look to Jesus Christ.

In the last year of his life (1662), Pascal sold all of his possessions and kept only the Bible and St. Augustine's *Confessions.* It seems a symbolic act by which this genius testified to what was important to his life. After all was said and done, Jesus Christ was the answer.

The edition of Pascal's *Pensées* translated by W. F. Trotter contains 923 selections from the author's notes and offers an excellent introduction by T. S. Eliot.

Hannah Whitall Smith, whose name was made famous by her book, *The Christian's Secret of a Happy Life,* was born in Philadelphia in 1832. Both of her parents had long associations with the Society of Friends so she was raised among conscientious Quakers who gave her a home life of broad culture and deep spiritual piety.

At the age of sixteen, Hannah Whitall had the first of what she describes as four religious epochs. This one, she admitted later, was a "period of morbid self-introspection." It lasted until her marriage, in 1851, to

Robert Pearsall Smith, who was a glass manufacturer by occupation and a religious author by avocation.

In 1858, Mrs. Smith passed through her second epoch when she came under the influence of the religious group called Plymouth Brethren. In this period, she found a new assurance about faith, a conviction which deepened in the succeeding years when she had two more religious epochs, the last of which moved her to write *The Christian's Secret,* which has since become so popular that it has been translated into almost every language.

She and her husband preached together and shared partnership in religious evangelism in many countries. Mrs. Smith was a practical speaker of wit and the Spirit, who worked strenuously for peace, temperance, and a widening influence of women.

She moved to England in 1886, where her husband died in 1898. She died at Iffley in 1905.

THE CHRISTIAN'S SECRET OF A HAPPY LIFE
Hannah Whitall Smith   1870

This is a joyful, personal, entertaining, and evangelistic testimony by a woman who has been touched by the Presence and who wants all of the world to enjoy her discovery.

Smith stresses that "Thy part is to yield thyself. His part is to work." Her enthusiastic romance with the Spirit is in three sections: (1) the invitation to yield; (2) meeting doubts, temptations, and failures; and (3) the practical spiritual rewards of yielding.

The book is in plain everyday language, dealing with everyday people. It is a joyous testimony that the truths of the Bible can be taken literally and will be fulfilled. Smith employs many excellent illustrations from daily life to make her appeal to yield to the Spirit most convincing. She has a holy optimism, touched with practical reality, that every person can enjoy a new life by accepting the promises of God.

The book avoids denominational differences and theologies. It is a personal conversation with the reader, constantly urging one to live the happy Christian life. It is a popular religious paperback which can be found in most bookstores.

Jeremy Taylor was born in Cambridge, England, the son of a well-educated barber, who ensured that his son have a good education. Thus, from his birth in 1613, Taylor was sent to a succession of good schools and colleges until he entered the Church of England as a young man in 1633.

The period into which Taylor moved as an adult was a time of extraordinary religious-political turbulence. King Charles I, through his archbishop, William Laud, was exerting control over the life of the Church—a political policy that brought war to both England and Scotland. Taylor was drawn into the struggle by Laud and later was appointed chaplain to both the archbishop and King Charles. But the position was unsafe and Taylor was put in prison on several occasions when the policies of the king suffered reversals. It was during these imprisonments that Taylor did much of his unusually fine literary work.

Most of his writings were concerned with contemporary

problems of Church and State and are of little interest today. However, he also wrote a number of devotional books that are among the most notable in the English language; among them are *Great Exemplar* (1649); *The Rule and Exercises of Holy Living* (1650); *The Rule and Exercises of Holy Dying* (1651); *Golden Grove* (1655); and *The Worthy Communicant* (1660).

The last part of his life was spent as vice-chancellor of the University of Dublin, until his death in Ireland in 1667.

THE RULE AND EXERCISES OF HOLY DYING
Jeremy Taylor 1651

This is a series of sober discourses written for Christians who had been excluded from the Church of England because of their Puritan convictions. The book is a manual of spiritual direction to help these laypersons officially administer to each other, during times of illness and death, when without benefit of clergy.

Taylor reminds the sick person of the shortness of life and then how he or she can prepare for a holy death. Next he discusses the temptations facing those who are ill, such as impatience and fear. He offers many prayers for patience. Finally, he gives directions for visiting the sick and helping at the time of death.

For Taylor, "Holy dying is an art to which each man must accustom himself before he loses his strength." He calls upon Christians to face death heroically.

Few devotional guides deal with the topic of death and how to face it. For this reason, the book is interesting and meaningful. However, Taylor writes in a flowery style, which makes the book difficult to read today.

THE RULE AND EXERCISES OF HOLY LIVING
Jeremy Taylor 1650

Ralph Waldo Emerson described Jeremy Taylor as "the Shakespeare of the divines." It was an appropriate title, for in England (in the seventeenth century) Taylor was recognized as a man of vast learning, and extraordinary skill at expressing religious matters in print. He wrote with a balanced Anglican sobriety and with an emphasis upon orderly piety. For him, Christian living required discipline.

This work deals with various concerns of the average person who is trying to cultivate the Presence: such as the proper use of time, the importance of chastity, humility, modesty, reading, and prayer. Each concern is followed by comments urging the reader to be more conscientious and God-fearing. The position taken by Taylor is that heaven is reserved for those who live in a holy manner. Most of the book, however, moralizes without specific examples, which makes it hard reading when taken in long sessions.

Nevertheless, the multitude of short essays on *Holy Living* challenges the reader to a more Christian life in a way that has remained popular with serious-minded men and women.

One of the great reformers of the Spanish Catholic Church, and today one of the patron saints of Spain, is *St. Teresa of Avila,* who was born in 1515 at Avila in Old Castile. Teresa was the oldest of ten children.

Her mother raised her in the influence of the Church, and later, over the objections of her father, she entered the

Carmelite Order at Avila. The lack of asceticism soon displeased her but she made no efforts at reform. However, a study of St. Augustine's *Confessions,* together with the beginning of religious visions, encouraged her to restore the Order to its original rigidness of conduct and servanthood. She withdrew and set up a new convent in which she put her own ideas into effect. In spite of much opposition, her reforms were approved by the pope; so much so, in fact, that they were soon extended to more and more convents. For twenty years, Teresa of Avila traveled throughout Spain implementing her reforms. *The Interior Castle* was used as a guide for better spiritual discipline.

She wrote an autobiography and a number of spiritual treatises. Her *Book of Foundations* describes, with many human anecdotes, how she established sixteen convents of the Carmelite Order during the last fifteen years of her life. The book is filled with illustrations of her courage, common sense, and spiritual power. Her *Way of Perfection* is a work of mystical beauty, which was written at the height of her reforms. It has much practical advice for safeguarding spiritual life against worldly temptations.

She died at Alba in 1582. In 1617, the Spanish Parliament proclaimed her the Patroness of Spain.

THE INTERIOR CASTLE
Teresa of Avila   1577

The Interior Castle, or *The Mansions* as its Spanish title translates, was written in 1577 as a spiritual guide for a group of nuns under Teresa, in the Discalced ("barefoot") Order of Carmelites in Spain. It was used in Teresa's reform program in convents and monasteries.

In the beginning of *The Interior Castle,* Teresa explains how she thinks of the human soul as a wonderful castle, made of a single diamond, with many rooms, just as in heaven there are many mansions. The door to the mansions is prayer.

In the First Mansion the soul is filled with worldly affairs, which are like wild beasts that force the pilgrim to keep his eyes closed to all but himself. The Second Mansion brings the pray-er closer to His Majesty through the reading of good books, sermons, and conversations with good people. The Third Mansion reveals the soul struggling with many ethical problems. As one progresses toward the Seventh Mansion, the seeker discovers the higher levels of prayer and Teresa leads the person further and further up to the highest summits of spiritual experience.

St. Teresa is too austere for most pilgrims today. She emphasizes otherworldliness. Except for seeking the souls of others, she has little interest in alleviating social conditions which might have caused those souls to be lost. Nevertheless, the book is a spiritual classic of much importance and value for personal religious development.

THE WAY OF PERFECTION
Teresa of Avila   1565

This guide to prayer was written at the height of the controversy over the reforms of monastic life, suggested by Teresa of Spain. The object of the book is to teach nuns the importance of prayer as the most effective way of attaining Christian virtue and Spirit.

The first chapters deal with counsels concerning the problems of human relationships in a convent. Later the author comments at length on vocal and mental prayer and contemplation. The second half of the book is a commentary on the Lord's Prayer.

Some of the concerns of *The Way* reflect the sixteenth century, such as ''Can a soul in grave sin enjoy supernatural contemplation?'' Most of the pages, however, present a personal appeal for a more disciplined Christian life.

Teresa of Avila was a mystic and also a practical spiritual genius. Her book is indeed a devotional classic, which will best be appreciated by the experienced religious.

The translation of E. Allison Peers, an authority on her writings, is excellent.

There is much controversy about *Thomas à Kempis* as an author. Some people claim that he was the writer of the devotional classic *Imitation of Christ*. Others hold that he was the editor and that Gerhard Groote, a Dutch mystic, wrote the book. While the debate continues, it is worthwhile to know that Thomas was born in 1380, in the town of Kempen, Holland. He was reared in a peasant home and received his education in the house-schools, which were creations of the Brethren of the Common Life, a movement for the better care of the poor, founded by Gerhard Groote and others. When Thomas was twenty-four years old he became a member of the Community at Mount St. Agnes, a fellowship of brethren.

Thomas à Kempis was ordained in 1414. As a priest he became a part of the problems of his time. For the next ten years he helped the sick and dying in the plague that was sweeping Europe. From 1425 to 1441, he served as copyist of the monastery Bible. Later he became involved in defending his fellow monks against the attacks of nearby notables, who were displeased about some ecclesiastical decisions.

Thomas never held high positions, but his career as a copyist enabled him also to be a writer. He wrote a number of devotional books, including *Meditation on Christ's Life, The Soul's Soliloquy,* and, we feel, *Imitation of Christ.* He died in 1471.

IMITATION OF CHRIST
Attributed to Thomas à Kempis   1418

With the exception of the Bible, the *Imitation* is the most influential spiritual guide of all Christendom. The number of editions exceeds two thousand, in more than fifty languages.

The author stresses how to be a different self instead of creating a better world. ''Conquer yourself where you are.'' His thesis is that the more one strips one's self of self-will, the closer one comes to God. This emphasis upon self-renunciation has led many critics to observe that the *Imitation* is too otherworldly and concerned only with the salvation of the individual.

The *Imitation* is filled with quotations from Holy Scripture. The first fourteen chapters of Book One are the most valuable for most Christians, because they deal with the preparatory instructions for the Christian life, while the remaining chapters of this book relate to matters of monastic life. Book Two deals with devotional living; Book Three with ''inward consolation''; and Book Four with Holy Communion.

No serious seeker of the Presence can go far without becoming familiar with this great devotional classic.

The most prolific British writer about the spiritual life was *Evelyn Underhill,* who was born into a wealthy home (her father's hobby was yachting) in England in 1875. Travels in Europe introduced her to a wide variety of interests from archaeology, flowers, and birds, to book binding. She also proved to be a keen student of languages and philosophy. But her main concern was the religious life, in which she was deeply involved when she married a lawyer named Stuart Moore in 1907. At the time of her marriage she had already written four books and was an insightful and witty lecturer.

In 1911, Evelyn Underhill (she continued to use this name as an author) wrote her most comprehensive work, *Mysticism,* which brought her into a search for deeper spirituality under the direction of the Italian mystic Baron von Hügel.

Following an exploration into the doctrines of the Catholic Church, she returned to the Church of England and began to include more of its teachings in her interpretation of the Spirit. In her final years, she spent most of her time writing and leading retreats, in which she stayed active even though she was often in poor health. She died in London in 1941.

In her lifetime, she wrote and edited thirty-seven books; among them were *The Life of the Spirit* (1922), *The Golden Sequence* (1932), *Worship* (1936), *The Spiritual Life* (1937), and *The Fruits of the Spirit* (1942).

THE GOLDEN SEQUENCE
Evelyn Underhill   1932

The Golden Sequence is a fourfold guide to the development of the spiritual life. Its four parts include (1) a description of what is meant by Spirit, plus illustrations of the Spirit as intervenor, power, and person; (2) a view of Man as natural as well as supernatural; with the love of God and the response of Man seeking to unite the two; (3) the need to purify the senses, the intellect, and even memory in order to know God; (4) the necessary steps in prayer in order to bring Man to communion and service with the Holy.

The book is filled with quotations from St. John of the Cross, Jan van Ruysbroeck, St. Francis of Assisi, Friedrich von Hügel, and other mystics. It is a religiously oriented, rational study of mystical reality, containing considerable theological material.

Underhill is a patient and thorough writer on the interior life. Her books are always clear in presentation and very rewarding. This book is more suitable for the advanced seeker than the beginner.

THE SPIRITUAL LIFE
Evelyn Underhill   1937

This is a short, but sublime, essay and personal testimony. Underhill describes the spiritual life as "a force beyond the world which breaks in upon the temporal order with disconcerting power," and a "source of that quality which makes practical life worthwhile."

This experienced author uses illustrations from history, from the Bible, and from contemporary living to reveal how the spiritual life is communion and cooperation with God. "We are agents of the Creative Spirit in this world. Real advance in the Spiritual Life, then, means accepting this vocation with all it involves."

The book has the spiritual depth of a psalm. It is an example of a devotional masterpiece.

The man who laid the foundations of the worldwide Methodist Church began his eventful life as the fifteenth child of Samuel and Susanna Wesley. Samuel was rector in Epworth, England when *John Wesley* was born in 1703. Thus John grew up in clerical poverty, but even so, he followed his father's calling and entered the ministry when he was twenty-one. For several years he continued to live a frivolous social life but then turned away from worldly distractions to follow a very disciplined existence. He began to study William Law, the author of *A Serious Call to a Devout and Holy Life,* whose writings led him into an even deeper commitment to religion.

In 1753, Wesley tried missionary work in America but did not find it spiritually rewarding. He returned to England where he came under the influence of the Moravians, a Protestant sect based on the teaching of the reformer John Huss. In 1738, at a meeting at Aldersgate, he had a conversion experience which renewed his whole life. He traveled more extensively (with his brother, Charles) but many churches were closed to him because of his new evangelistic spirit. So he spoke in fields and open-air meetings, drawing large crowds. He wrote copiously with methodical emphasis upon faith and worship. In later years he organized lay preachers.

After a strenuous life, traveling, speaking, organizing, challenging, suffering, and testifying for his Lord, Wesley died in 1791, in his eighty-eighth year.

JOURNAL
John Wesley   1739

John Wesley began keeping a diary during his student days at Oxford, England. During his lifetime, he added twenty-one installments. The whole *Journal* consists of eight large volumes.

The principal ideas developed in the *Journal* are that the work of God is sometimes accompanied by emotional upheavals, that Christians need to gather together in small groups for mutual support, and that economic and social needs are an important concern for such groups.

Much of the *Journal* reports on answers to prayers and the healing power of faith. It is a daily record of Wesley's journeys and everyday experiences.

Many critics do not include the writings of John Wesley in a summary of mystics. Yet there can be no doubt but that he had felt the Presence and testified successfully to the power of God in the midst of multitudes of real-life difficulties.

The complete *Journal*, or smaller editions thereof, reveal the spiritual convictions which became the foundations for the Methodist Church.

A PLAIN ACCOUNT OF CHRISTIAN PERFECTION
John Wesley   1777

The *Journal* of John Wesley reports his daily spiritual adventures. *Christian Perfection* reflects his theology of holiness. Wesley believed according to the Scripture: "You must be perfect as your heavenly Father is perfect."

Christian Perfection is mostly a series of questions and answers, such as, "Can one that is saved from sin be tempted?" (Yes). . . . "Can those who are perfect grow in grace?" (Undoubtedly). . . . "Can they fall from it?" (They can).

Wesley held that there is such a thing as Christian perfection, though he felt it was not absolute and did not make a person infallible. He felt it was capable of being lost and was often a process of gradual development, though it could come instantaneously.

As in all his reports, Wesley writes for and to the everyday person. This book covers his theological explorations from 1725, when he first read Bishop Taylor's *The Rule and Exercises of Holy Living,* to 1777. (He died in 1791).

Christian Perfection will raise many questions of theology for the layman.

It is better for this use than as a devotional.

One of the most typical of all Quakers, because he reflected the Quaker spirit so thoroughly, was *John Woolman,* who was born into a Quaker community in New Jersey in 1720, and educated in a Quaker school.

A most important event in his life, in his eyes, was the moment when his Quaker Meeting endorsed his desire to be a minister by "recording" him at the age of twenty-three. Within a few years he was visiting small settlements, on behalf of the Quakers, in isolated rural sections of Virginia and neighboring areas.

Woolman began his personal religious *Journal* when he was thirty-six years old. Ellery Channing (who led the efforts to form the Unitarian Church in America) described it as "the sweetest and purest autobiography in the language."

From the very beginning of his life, Woolman had a sensitivity to social problems. In the year he began his Quaker work, he was asked to help write a bill of sale for a Negro slave. He refused. From then on, he spoke against slavery; sometimes leaving homes of hosts where slaves were held. As early as 1760, he urged a Yearly Meeting to petition the legislature to eliminate the slave trade.

Woolman traveled widely throughout his life, opposing the draft and taxation for military needs and speaking for better conditions for the poor and conversion of the Indians. While on a trip to England, his courageous Quaker testimony was cut short by smallpox in York, in 1772.

JOURNAL
John Woolman   1774

John Woolman's *Journal* is a good example of the Quaker attitude toward life, and the diary-keeping procedure employed by many religious persons during the flowering of Quakerism in America in the eighteenth century. It is a travel narrative and a dramatic statement of conscience.

Woolman tells about his family in a brief way. Only twelve pages of the *Journal* are used to describe the first thirty-six years of his life. He gives more attention to his early rejection of the opportunity to become successful in business. He tells of his dislike of the slave trade, his missions to the Indians, the spirit of Quaker meetings, and the social conditions of his times. This autobiography covers the years from 1743 to his death in 1772.

Woolman presents his differences with traditional society in the humble, thoughtful, and personal ways of a Quaker. The book is written in a clear and readable manner. One of his main points is that a person should live by the light of his own conscience, no matter what other people may think. He documents how a God-fearing conscience can confront and change unjust social conditions.

THE CLOUD OF UNKNOWING
Author Unknown   ca. 1375

An unidentified English monk wrote this book of contemplation to provide a psychologically penetrating and practical guide for the layperson who seeks a direct relationship with God.

The author takes the position that people should not rely on or use either memory or tradition to seek the Presence, for they are obstacles to the attainment of God and are dissipations of mental energy. He holds that contemplative practices which empty the mind of thought and reason are the best way to bring forth the powers of the Spirit. He says, "The task of the mystic is to bring his understanding to a halt in a cloud of unknowing, and then wait in that state for God to show himself."

Although the text is often veiled and many meanings are hidden from the novice, this work has taken on new meanings in our modern era of psychology. The translation by Ira Progoff is specially recommended, because of his helpful introductory comments and excellent translation of the original text. *The Cloud* is not recommended for the novice.

THEOLOGIA GERMANICA
Author Unknown   ca. 1350

"German Theology," an obscure little book of the middle fourteenth century, has become an important part of Protestant devotional literature.

The subject matter is derived from the Friends of God movement, which flourished along the Rhine River. Although the name of the author is not known, he was a Teutonic knight and, later, a priest. The book contains fifty-four chapters of informal conversations with young monks. It stresses obedience to Christ and says that present selfishness is the cause of sin and unhappiness. "As long as there is self-will, there will be no peace, true love or true rest." In pursuing this position, it often quotes the New Testament.

Martin Luther edited an edition in 1516, and hundreds of editions of this work have appeared since. It is a favorite among pietists. It is a classic of mystical literature. Those who seek the Presence should make the acquaintance of this book for spiritual growth.

The Place of Each Devotional Book in History

The appearance of spiritual-life books has been a recurring event in Christian literature. Each period produces its own authorities, and century after century, the list continues to grow.

While the fourteenth and fifteenth centuries witnessed the flowering of mysticism in such movements as the Brethren of the Common Life and the Friends of God, out of which came such timeless classics as *Imitation of Christ* and

Theologia Germanica, the publication of superb literature-of-the-Spirit has been a constant event in every generation of believers.

The following listing will give you a bird's-eye view of the historical-time relationship each author has had with the others.

Chronology of Authors

Name	Dates	Country of origin
Augustine of Hippo	354–430	North Africa
Bernard of Clairvaux	1090–1153	France
Francis of Assisi	1182–1226	Italy
Meister Eckhart	1260–1328	Germany
Catherine of Siena	1347–1380	Italy
Thomas à Kempis	1379–1471	Germany
Walter Hilton	?–1395	England
Martin Luther	1473–1546	Germany
Ignatius Loyola	1490–1556	Spain
Teresa of Avila	1515–1582	Spain
John of the Cross	1542–1591	Spain
Lancelot Andrewes	1555–1626	England
Francis de Sales	1567–1622	France
John Donne	1573–1630	England
Jacob Boehme	1575–1624	Germany
Brother Lawrence	1605–1691	France
Jeremy Taylor	1613–1667	England
Blaise Pascal	1623–1662	France
George Fox	1624–1691	England
John Bunyan	1628–1688	England
François Fénelon	1651–1715	France
Jean-Pierre de Caussade	1675–1751	France

Chronology of Authors–continued

Name	Dates	Country of origin
William Law	1686–1761	England
John Wesley	1703–1791	England
John Woolman	1720–1772	United States
Søren Kierkegaard	1813–1855	Denmark
Hannah Whitall Smith	1832–1911	United States
Friedrich von Hügel	1852–1925	Italy
Evelyn Underhill	1875–1941	England
Emily Herman	1876–1923	England
Teilhard de Chardin	1881–1955	France
John Baillie	1886–1960	England
Georgia Harkness	1891–1974	United States
Thomas R. Kelly	1893–1941	United States
Dietrich Bonhoeffer	1906–1945	Germany
Thomas Merton	1915–1968	United States

7

FINAL
REFLECTIONS

If you look, in perspective, at the programs of the churches and the activities of most Christians over the past century, you will discover that they have been involved in a variety of changing causes.

Around 1900, the American pulpit was urging our parents and grandparents to send money and missionaries to foreign lands. How exciting it must have been to help fulfill the call of the gospel by sending "ambassadors for Christ" "into all the world." Many believed the new twentieth century was going to be the Christian Century.

Then, for various reasons, interests changed and the Sunday School, with special programs of Christian Education, became the new Christian Cause: "Train up a child in the way he should go and when he is old he will not depart from it." The Scriptures seemed to encourage local parishes to use the closely graded lessons and uniform study material. Conversion was going to be taught as well as caught.

Still another emphasis came with the turbulent years of the midcentury. There was the anguished cry for integration, as racial equality, the right to vote, and equal opportunity became the new battle issues. "Get involved" was heard from almost every pulpit, or so it seemed. Some churches and some Christians grew with the challenge while others were torn apart by bitter controversy.

Now all of these causes are history, as we move yet again into a different effort, the Human Potential Movement, in which understanding of Self is paramount. Christians gather in small-group self-discovery sessions; therapy in many forms is popular; and books on learning how to be a free person flood the market.

It will be something else tomorrow, you can be sure of that!

Like thousands of others, I have asked myself, "What can I believe that will not be soon out of date? What is there about the Christian faith that will be permanent?" The more I asked these questions, the more I became aware of the life of interior spirituality: prayer, confession, patience, worship, willingness to suffer for the sake of others, devotion, humility, meditation, and love. Such religious principles are as unchanging as the human nature of which they are so deeply a part. Here are matters of the soul that remain vital in any generation. In the fourth century, St. Augustine struggled to master them, as did John Wesley in the eighteenth century. You and I are confronted with these same Christian fundamentals. Our children and grandchildren will meet them too.

I am not suggesting for a moment that we ignore missions, Christian education, social concern, or the development of the self.

I am suggesting that we consider more carefully the grounds upon which these movements have been founded. Each is a product of deep spiritual conviction. Each is a means by which faith is expressed. Each is a method to put the gospel into the world. Each is a work expressing faith.

I wish we always recognized this fact. Unfortunately we do not. Too often we become active in a Christian cause and overlook its spiritual roots. Too often we commit ourselves to meeting obvious needs and forget to nourish the Christian motivations needed to continue the effort to fulfill those needs. Too often we become engrossed in the unfolding beauty of a plant and fail to nourish the ground upon which its life and growth depends. For example, the activist may respond with enthusiasm to a program for a better environment, but may soon weaken in interest when the going gets rough if his or her commitment is just based on the belief that it is "the right thing to do." On the other hand, if he or she believes that participation in the campaign is in keeping with God's plan for a cleaner world, the enthusiasm has stronger roots and the determination to see it through has more power.

So I am not appealing for another cause. It will come along with regularity as the world demands new interpretations of the gospel for different eras. I am appealing for a more conscious acknowledgment of the Presence of God in every cause we undertake in Christ's name. I am concerned that churches, now so overprogrammed with activities, give deeper attention to matters of the soul and spirit. I am impressed that we need a far better balance between our materialistic living and our undernourished souls, and I am convinced that more cultivation of the Presence will rectify that present imbalance. I am concerned that more Americans permeate their living with a respect for the Maker of Life.

The cultivation of the Presence has provided tremendous power to Christians in previous ages, as I have illustrated, to such an extent that they have changed the course of history in their times. A renewed cultivation of the Presence today could significantly fulfill the plan of God more fully in our time.

Finally, I have sought, in this book, to establish three spiritual truths upon which your life can be built:

First, *that the Presence of God is as much a fact of life as breathing.* It can come to you anytime and anywhere. It is the supernatural intervention of God in His or Her effort to continue the plan of creation of which each of us, by being created in the image of God, is a part. This intervention of the Presence may come in the form of forgiveness, redirection to our lives, judgment, joy over sorrow, or love over hatred, as well as a multitude of other ways. I have described a number of ways by which this is continually happening to all sorts of people.

Second, *that although we cannot command the Presence of God, nevertheless we can cultivate It.*

As with the seed,
so with the Presence.

God alone can give It life,
I can only cultivate It.

It is my responsibility,
to use the best tools I know.

Each of us can cultivate the Presence in our lives by adopting attitudes and practicing principles which have been distilled from hundreds of years of spiritual seeking. I have suggested who some of the spiritual leaders are, and I have listed many of their best methods, as well as books, for your use.

Third, *that a closer relationship with the Presence should not turn anyone toward Self to the exclusion of the needs of his or her neighbor.* Indeed, the fullness and joy of the Christian is only discovered when interior faith and exterior works are in balance. Faith and works must complement each other for either to be valid. A good example of this, if not the best one in all of Christian literature, is the statement of purpose which Jesus Christ made when He first spoke in the sanctuary at the very beginning of His ministry:

The Spirit of the Lord is upon me,
because He has anointed me
to preach good news to the poor.
He has sent me to proclaim

release to the captives
and recovery of sight to the blind,
to set at liberty those who are oppressed,
to proclaim the acceptable year of the Lord.

Luke 4:18–19

Such a balance between faith and works should be the goal for all Christians.

EPILOGUE

Above all things, Philothea, when you rise from meditation, remember the resolutions you have taken and, as the occasion offers, carefully reduce them to practice that very day.

This is the great fruit of meditation, without which it is not only unprofitable, but frequently hurtful; for virtues meditated upon, and not practised often puff up the spirit, and make us imagine that we really are such as we resolve to be, which doubtless is true, when our resolutions are lively and solid; now they are not so, but, on the contrary vain and dangerous when they are not reduced to practice.

We must, therefore, by all means, seek every occasion, little or great, of putting them in execution.

St. Francis de Sales*

*Francis de Sales, *Introduction to a Devout Life* (Cleveland: World, 1952), Part 2, VIII, p. 95.

BIBLIOGRAPHY

Andrewes, Lancelot, *The Private Prayers of Lancelot Andrewes,* ed. Hugh Martin. London: SCM Press, 1957.

Atkin, Gaius, *Pilgrims on a Lonely Road.* Chicago: Revell, 1913.

Augustine, St., *Confessions,* tr. F. J. Sheed. New York: Sheed & Ward, 1942.

Baillie, John, *Christian Devotion.* New York: Scribner's, 1962.

————, *A Diary of Private Prayer.* Nashville: Abingdon, 1975.

————, *A Diary of Readings.* New York: Scribner's, 1955.

Baker, James T., *Thomas Merton, Social Critic.* Lexington: University of Kentucky Press, 1971.

Bernard of Clairvaux, *On Consideration,* tr. G. Lewis. New York: Oxford University Press, 1908.

————, *The Steps of Humility,* tr. George B. Burch. Cambridge, Mass.: Harvard University Press, 1942.

Boehme, Jacob, *The Confessions of Jacob Boehme,* ed. W. Scott Palmer. New York: Harper & Bros., 1954.

Bonhoeffer, Dietrich, *Letters and Papers from Prison,* tr. Reginald Ruller et al. New York: Macmillan paperback, enlarged edition, 1972.

Bunyan, John, *Grace Abounding to the Chief of Sinners.* Chicago: Allenson, 1955.

————, *Pilgrim's Progress.* New York: Dutton, 1972.

Caussade, Jean-Pierre de, *Abandonment to Divine Providence,* tr. John Beevers. Garden City, N.Y.: Doubleday, 1975.

Dillenberger, John, *Martin Luther.* Garden City, N.Y.: Doubleday, 1961.

Donne, John, *Devotions upon Emergent Occasions.* Ann Arbor: University of Michigan Press, 1965.

Eckhart, Meister, *Meister Eckhart,* tr. Raymond Blakney. New York: Harper & Bros., 1957.

Edwards, Jonathan, *Religious Affections,* ed. John E. Smith. New Haven: Yale University Press, 1959.

Fénelon, François, *Christian Perfection,* tr. Mildred W. Stillman. New York: Harper & Bros., 1947.

——, *A Guide to True Peace.* New York: Harper & Bros., 1946.

——, *Letters of Love and Counsel,* tr. John McEwen. New York: Harper & Row, 1964.

Ferre, Nels, *Strengthening the Spiritual Life.* New York: Harper & Bros., 1947.

Fox, George, *Journal,* ed. Thomas S. Kepler. Nashville: Upper Room, 1951.

Francis de Sales, *Introduction to a Devout Life,* ed. Thomas S. Kepler. Cleveland: World, 1952.

Francis of Assisi, *Little Flowers of St. Francis,* tr. and ed. Raphael Brown. Garden City, N.Y.: Doubleday, 1971.

Grou, Jean Nicholas, *Manual for Interior Souls.* New York: Benziger, 1932.

Harkness, Georgia, *Dark Night of the Soul.* Nashville: Abingdon, 1968.

——, *Mysticism.* Nashville: Abingdon, 1973.

Herman, Emily, *Creative Prayer.* New York: Harper & Bros., 1940.

Hilton, Walter, *The Scale of Perfection,* tr. Leo Sherley-Price. St. Meinrad, Ind.: Abbey Press, 1975.

Hügel, Friedrich von, *Spiritual Counsel and Letters,* ed. Douglas Steere. London: Longmans, 1964.

James, William, *Varieties of Religious Experience.* New York: Random House, 1929.

John of the Cross, *Dark Night of the Soul,* tr. and ed. E. Allison Peers. Garden City, N.Y.: Doubleday, 1959.

Jones, Rufus, *The Flowering of Mysticism.* New York: Macmillan, 1939.

————, *Spiritual Reformers of the Sixteenth Century*. Boston: Beacon, 1959.

Julian of Norwich, *Revelations of Divine Love,* tr. James Walsh. St. Meinrad, Ind.: Abbey Press, 1974.

Kaplan, Nathaniel, *The Western Mystical Tradition*. New Haven: Yale University Press, 1969.

Kelly, Thomas R. *A Testament of Devotion*. New York: Harper & Bros., 1941.

Kepler, Thomas S., ed., *The Evelyn Underhill Reader*. Nashville: Abingdon, 1962.

————, *Leaves from a Spiritual Notebook*. Nashville: Abingdon, 1970.

Kierkegaard, Søren, *Purity of Heart Is to Will One Thing,* tr. Douglas Steere. New York: Harper & Bros., 1938.

————, *The Prayers of Kierkegaard,* ed. Perry Le Fevre. Chicago: University of Chicago Press, 1956.

Law, William, *Christian Perfection,* ed. Erwin Paul Rudolph. Carol Stream, Ill.: Creation House, 1975.

————, *A Serious Call to a Devout and Holy Life,* ed. John W. Meister. Philadelphia: Westminster Press, 1975.

Lawrence, Brother, *The Practice of the Presence of God*. Old Tappan, N.J.: Revell, 1895.

Loyola, Ignatius, *Spiritual Exercises,* tr. Thomas Corbishley. Garden City, N.Y.: Doubleday, 1964.

McNeill, John T., *Books of Faith and Power*. New York: Harper & Bros., 1947.

Merton, Thomas, *Contemplation in a World of Action*. Garden City, N.Y.: Doubleday, 1971.

————, *Spiritual Direction and Meditation*. Collegeville, Minn.: Liturgical Press, 1959.

Miller, Samuel, *Life of the Soul*. New York: Harper & Bros., 1951.

O'Connor, Elizabeth, *Search for Silence*. Waco, Tex.: Word, 1974.

————, *Journey Inward, Journey Outward*. New York: Harper & Row, 1968.

Progoff, Ira, tr., *The Cloud of Unknowing.* New York: Dell, 1973.

Rahner, Karl, *Encounters with Silence,* tr. James Demske. Westminster, Md.: Newman Press, 1960.

————, *On Prayer.* Westminster, Md.: Paulist-Newman, 1965.

————, *Spirit in the World,* tr. William Dych. New York: Herder & Herder, 1968.

Sitwell, Gerard, *Spiritual Writers of the Middle Ages.* New York: Hawthorn, 1961.

Smith, Hannah Whitall, *The Christian's Secret of a Happy Life.* Old Tappan, N.J.: Revell, 1970.

Stace, Willard T., *The Teaching of the Mystics.* New York: Mentor, 1960.

————, *Mysticism and Philosophy.* New York: Lippincott, 1960.

Steere, Douglas, *On Beginning from Within.* New York: Harper & Bros., 1943.

————, *Work and Contemplation.* New York: Harper & Bros., 1957.

Tauler, Johannes, *Discourses on the Interior Life.* Old Tappan, N.J.: Revell, 1970.

Taylor, Jeremy, *The Rule and Exercises of Holy Dying.* Cleveland: World, 1956.

————, *The Rule and Exercises of Holy Living.* Cleveland: World, 1956.

Teilhard de Chardin, Pierre, *The Divine Milieu,* tr. Bernard Wall et al. New York: Harper & Bros., 1960.

Teresa of Avila, *The Interior Castle.* Garden City, N.Y.: Doubleday, 1972.

————, *The Way of Perfection,* tr. and ed. E. Allison Peers. Garden City, N.Y.: Doubleday, 1972.

Thomas à Kempis, *Imitation of Christ,* ed. Thomas S. Kepler. Cleveland: World, 1956.

Thurman, Howard, *The Inward Journey.* New York: Harper & Bros., 1961.

Underhill, Evelyn, *Concerning the Inner Life.* London: Methuen, 1947.

————, *The Golden Sequence*. New York: Harper & Bros., 1960.

————, *Meditation and Prayers*. New York: Longmans, 1949.

————, *Mysticism*. Cleveland: World, 1970.

Wesley, John, *Journal*, ed. P. L. Parker. Chicago: Moody, 1974.

————, *A Plain Account of Christian Perfection*, ed. Thomas S. Kepler. Cleveland: World, 1954.

Woolman, John, *Journal*. New York: Corinth, 1968.

Wyon, Olive, *The School of Prayer*. Philadelphia: Westminster, 1944.

ANTHOLOGIES

It has become popular, when classic books of the spiritual life are written about, to present them in the form of anthologies. Such a method offers the reader a wide selection of resources as well as a fine perspective on the varieties of spiritual life.

Barrois, George, ed., *Pathways of the Inner Life*. New York: Bobbs-Merrill, 1956. (Thirty-three excerpts from as many authors.)

Christensen, Bernard, *The Inward Pilgrimage*. Minneapolis: Augsburg, 1976. (The Desert Fathers, St. Teresa, Kierkegaard, E. Herman, Hallesby, Underhill, and others.)

Fremantle, Anne, *The Protestant Mystics*. Boston: Little, Brown, 1964. (An excellent survey of the field from a Protestant point of view.)

Harkness, Georgia, *A Devotional Treasury from the Early Church*. Nashville: Abingdon, 1968. (First Clement, Polycarp, Shepherd of Hermas, The Didache, the Odes of Solomon, and others.)

Hinson, E. Glenn, *Seekers after Mature Faith*. Waco, Tex.: Word, 1968. (An excellent appraisal of the major "spiritual life" persons from the first to the twentieth century.)

Kepler, Thomas S., *The Fellowship of the Saints*. Nashville: Abingdon, 1958. (A large book offering a wide introduction to the writings of most well-known authors in this field.)

Peers, Edgar A., *Behind That Wall*. London: SCM Press, 1947. (Excerpts from Augustine, Bernard, Teresa, Waughan, St. John, Trahuerne, and others.)

Phillips, Dorothy Berkley, *The Choice Is Always Ours*. New York: Harper & Bros., 1960. (Excerpts on the Religious Way from psychological, religious, philosophical, and biographical sources.)

Sperry, Willard, *Classics of Religious Devotion*. Boston: Beacon, 1950. (Augustine, Kempis, Bunyan, Woolman, Schweitzer.)

Steere, Douglas, *Doors into Life*. New York: Harper & Bros., 1948. (Kempis, de Sales, Woolman, Kierkegaard, von Hügel.)

Steere, Douglas, ed., *The Very Thought of Thee*. Nashville: The Upper Room, 1953. (Bernard of Clairvaux, Taylor, Underhill.)

Williams, Michael, *The Book of Christian Classics*. New York: Liveright, 1943. (Augustine, Sculpoli, Ruysbroeck, Law, Newman, Patmor, and others.)

INDEX

Boldface page numbers indicate biographies of authors

Hilton, Walter (*continued*)
  The Scale of Perfection, review,
    157
Hügel, Friedrich von, **157**
  on cultivation, 31
  on devotions, 37
  on dryness, 51
  Selected Letters, review, 158

Imitation of Christ (Kempis):
  excerpt, 97
  recommended, 126
  review, 179
individual responsibility, 111
Inner Light of the Quakers, 30
inner spiritual conflict of:
  Augustine, Saint, 80, 130
  Boehme, Jacob, 81, 104
  Bunyan, John, 81
  Fox, George, 95
  Lawrence, Brother, 106
  Paul, Saint, 23, 79
  Teresa, Saint, 80
  Woolman, John, 118
Interior Castle, The (Teresa of Avila), 176

John of the Cross, **159**
  Dark Night of the Soul, review,
    160
Journal:
  (Fox), 95, 148
  (Wesley), 183
  (Woolman), 185
joy, perfect, 108

Kelly, Thomas R., **161**
  on cultivation, steps of, 33
  on the Divine Center, vii

Kelly, Thomas R. (*continued*)
  on prayer, continuous, 46
  A Testament of Devotion, review, 162
Kepler, Thomas S., 87
Kierkegaard, Søren, 75, **162**
  Purity of Heart, excerpt, 111
  Purity of Heart, review, 163

Law, William, **164**
  Christian Perfection, review,
    165
  on cultivation, place for, 32
  on cultivation, time for, 36
  on prayer, importance of, 46
  *A Serious Call to a Devout and
    Holy Life,* review, 166
Lawrence, Brother, **166**
  early life of, ix
  *The Practice of the Presence of
    God,* excerpt, 106
  *The Practice of the Presence of
    God,* review, 167
  prayer life secret of, 40
Life of the Spirit, The (Underhill),
  92
Life Together (Bonhoeffer), 137
"Light within" of George Fox,
  19, 30
Little Flowers of St. Francis, 108,
  151
love of others, test of, 110
Loyola, Ignatius, 30, **168**
  Spiritual Exercises, review, 169
Luther, Martin, 45
  Freedom of a Christian, The,
    excerpt, 112
  Sermons on the Catechism, excerpt, 120

Martha and Mary, 65
Merton, Thomas:
    on a guide, need for, 34
    on meditation, 55–60
    on social action, 70
    on soul and mind, compared, 76
missions, 192
mother of St. Peter, legend of, 27
mysticism, defined, 124

On Consideration (Bernard of
    Clairvaux), 102

Pascal, Blaise, 74, **169**
    Pensées, review, 184
Paul, Saint:
    conversion of, 23
    inner conflict of, 79
Pensées (Pascal), 184
perfection, attainment of, 117
Personal experiences of author,
    1–16
piety, personal, 64
Pilgrim's Progress (Bunyan), 99,
    139
*Practice of the Presence of God,
    The* (Brother Lawrence), ix,
    106, 167
prayer (see also *Creative Prayer; A
    Diary of Private Prayer; Pri-
    vate Prayers*):
    answers to, 53
    by Baillie, 89
    and daily activity, 46
    discipline of, 47
    by Fénelon, 49
    importance of, 40
    introduction to, 44
    by Lawrence, Brother, 7, 48
    by Pascal, 74

prayer (*continued*)
    positive vs. negative, 53
    posture in, 47
    purpose of, 52
    and self-improvement, 47
    time for, 49
    by Thomas à Kempis, 97
Presence, the:
    categories of, 18
    description of, xi ff.
    experience of, 18
    as Grace, state of, 20
    guarantees of, lacking, 73
    human nature and, 25
    inescapability of, 21, 22
    inner security of, 20
    intervention of, 22
    practice of, 106
    social responsibility and, 27
    test of, 103
    unseen energy of, 25
Private Prayers (Andrewes), 130
Protestants and Catholics, com-
    pared, 77
Purity of Heart (Kierkegaard),
    111, 163

racial equality, 192
readings:
    best twelve, listed, 126
    collections of, recommended,
      86
    criteria for selections in this
      book, 124
    devotional, examples of, 55
    devotional, how to use, 56
    excerpts from, in this book,
      listed, 87 ff.
    reviews of, in this book, listed,
      127 ff.

responsibility for society:
  and Bonhoeffer, Dietrich, 136
  and Eckhart, Meister, 69
  and Fox, George, 147
  and Francis de Sales, 69, 197
  and Francis of Assisi, 109, 150
  and Kelly, Thomas, 161
  and Merton, Thomas, 70
  and Underhill, Evelyn, 69, 73
  and Woolman, John, 118, 184
religious growth, steps in, 41 ff.
Rule and Exercise of Holy Dying,
  The, (Taylor), 174
Rule and Exercise of Holy Living,
  The, (Taylor), 101, 175
Ruysbroeck, Jan, on discipline, 43

sanctification, personal, 64
Scale of Perfection, The (Hilton),
  110, 157
Selected Letters (Hügel), 158
self:
  begin with your own, 103
  personal concern for, 102, 111
  victory over, 75
Serious Call to a Devout and Holy
  Life, A (Law), 166
Sermons on the Catechism
  (Luther), 120
silence:
  Quakers and, 60
  solitude and, 60
Smith, Hannah Whitall, **171**
  The Christian's Secret of a
    Happy Life, excerpt, 115
  The Christian's Secret of a
    Happy Life, review, 172
Song of Songs, The (Bernard of
  Clairvaux), 103

Spiritual Exercises, The (Loyola),
  169
spiritual growth, steps in, 41 ff.
spiritual guide, need for, 34
Spiritual Life, The (Underhill), 92,
  181
Steere, Douglas, 57

Taylor, Jeremy, 36, **173**
  The Rule and Exercises of Holy
    Dying, review, 175
  The Rule and Exercises of Holy
    Living, excerpt, 101
  The Rule and Exercises of Holy
    Living, review, 175
temptations of:
  Augustine, Saint, 80
  Boehme, Jacob, 104
  Fox, George, 95
  Paul, Saint, 79
  Teresa, Saint, 80
Teresa of Avila, Saint, 47, 80, **175**
  The Interior Castle, review, 176
  The Way of Perfection, review,
    177
Testament of Devotion, A (Kelly),
  162
Theologia Germanica (anony-
  mous):
  basic disciplines from, 42
  excerpt, 117
  review, 187
Thomas à Kempis, **178**
  Imitation of Christ, excerpt, 97
  Imitation of Christ, review, 179
time:
  amount of, for devotions, 37
  spiritual investment in, 36
  spiritual miracle of, 37

COPYRIGHT

ACKNOWLEDGMENTS

Grateful acknowledgment is made to the following copyright holders for permission to use their material:

Abingdon Press for the quotation from *The Fellowship of the Saints,* ed. Thomas S. Kepler, copyright © 1948, by Thomas S. Kepler.

Corinth Press for the quotation from *The Journal of John Woolman,* The John Greenleaf Whittier Edition, copyright © 1968 by The Corinth Press.

Crown Publishers, Inc., for the quotation from *The Cloud of Unknowing,* tr. Ira Progoff. English translation © 1957 by Ira Progoff.

Doubleday & Co., Inc., for the quotation from *Little Flowers of St. Francis,* tr. and ed. Raphael Brown, copyright © 1958 by Beverly H. Brown; for the quotation from *Martin Luther,* copyright © 1961 by Joseph Dillenberger.

Fortress Press for quotations from *Luther's Works:* Vol. 31, *Career of the Reformer, I,* tr. W. A. Lambert, ed. and rev. Harold J. Grimm, copyright © 1957 by Fortress Press; Vol. 51, *Sermons, I,* tr. John W. Doberstein, ed. Helmut T. Lehmann, copyright © 1959 by Fortress Press.

Harper & Row, Publishers, for the quotation from *The Confessions of Jacob Boehme,* ed. W. Scott Palmer; for the quotation from Søren Kierkegaard, *Purity of Heart Is to Will One Thing,* tr. Douglas Steere, copyright 1938, 1948 by Harper & Bros.; and for the quotations from *A Testament of Devotion* by Thomas R. Kelly, copyright 1941 by Harper & Bros.

Liturgical Press, copyrighted by The Order of St. Benedict, Inc., Collegeville, Minn., for the quotations from Thomas Merton, *Spiritual Direction and Meditation.*

Mowbray Co., Alden Press, for the quotation from Bernard of Clairvaux, *The Song of Songs,* tr. anonymously, copyright © 1952 by A. R. Mowbray & Co., Ltd.

Thomas Nelson & Sons, for the short quotations from *The Holy Bible, Revised Standard Version.*

Oxford University Press for the quotation from Bernard of Clairvaux, *On Consideration,* tr. G. Lewis.

Fleming H. Revell Co. for the quotations from *The Practice of the Presence of God* by Brother Lawrence; *The Christian's Secret of a Happy Life* by Hannah Whitall Smith, and *Pilgrim's Progress* by John Bunyan.

Charles Scribner's Sons, for the quotation from John Baillie's *Christian Devotion,* copyright © 1962 by F. Jewel Baillie; Scribner's and Oxford University Press, Oxford, for the quotation from "First Day—Morning" from John Baillie's *A Diary of Private Prayer,* copyright 1949 by Charles Scribner's Sons.

Sheed & Ward, Inc., for the quotation from St. Augustine, *Confessions,* tr. F. J. Sheed; copyright 1943, Sheed & Ward, Inc., New York.

The Upper Room, for the quotation from George Fox's *Journal,* copyright © 1951 by The Upper Room.

Westminster Press, for the quotation from Georgia Harkness, *A Devotional Treasury from the Early Church,* for a selection originally included in *Early Christian Fathers,* Vol. 1, The Library of Christian Classics, newly tr. and ed. Cyril C. Richardson. Published in the United States by The Westminster Press, 1953.

W. H. N. Wilkinson for the U.S. rights and Associated Book Publishers, Ltd., London, for the Canadian rights to the quotation from Evelyn Underhill, *The Life of the Spirit and the Life Today,* published by Methuen & Co., Ltd., London.

Geoffrey Chapman, a division of Cassell and Collier-Macmillan Publishers, Ltd., for material from *The Scale of Perfection* by Walter Hilton.

The Christian Century Foundation for material from Section D, pages 11–14 of this book, reprinted from *The Christian Ministry,* Sept. 1975, copyright © 1975 by Christian Century Foundation.